Praise for THE DIGITAL ALCHEMIST®

"*The Digital Alchemist®* is a compelling and well-written guide for those who are on the cusp of major business change. Eric Marcus opens a portal to the leading edge based on his field consulting work with many of the largest businesses on the planet. In that role he has devised many frameworks, thought processes and strategies which he shares in this book to avoid the catastrophes awaiting those who do not heed the warning signs."

— Susan Annunzio, recognized authority in the field of change management and author of business bestseller, *Evolutionary Leadership: Dynamic Ways to Make Your Corporate Culture Fast and Flexible*

"Eric Marcus manages to make technology and its strategic impacts understandable to business people — which is a hard trick to pull off. He offers practical recommendations and immediate insights to make your business more successful."

— Jennifer Allerton, Chief Information Officer, Roche Pharmaceuticals

"I can guarantee that you will find something in *The Digital Alchemist®* that will change the way you see and think of the world of technology and business. So many business books can tell you what happened yet, so very few can give us a glimpse of what is to come and what should be done. Eric Marcus is a consummate observer and experimenter in the field of business and strategy and I found valuable food for thought, new perspectives and insights in this book."

— Peter Cochrane, Founder and CEO, ConceptLabs and former Chief Technology Officer, British Telecommunications

"Eric Marcus really understands the strategic thinking process! I applaud his insightful way of not only helping organizations succeed in the future but in truly redefining their futures in light of the information age."

— Nancy Wilson Smith, Senior Vice President, National Association of Realtors®

THE DIGITAL ALCHEMIST®

The Digital Alchemist:® Strategies to Transform Your Organization into Information Age Gold by Eric Marcus

Published by Strategic Vision Press.

Cover and interior design and production by Pneuma Books:
The premier book development and marketing solution for publishers.
www.pneumadesign.com/books/info.htm

First Edition

Printed in the United States of America by Thomson-Shore, Dexter, MI

10 9 8 7 6 5 4 3 2 1   10 09 08 07 06 05 04 03 02

Publisher's Cataloging-in-Publication Data

Marcus, Eric
The Digital Alchemist: Strategies to Transform Your Organization into Information Age Gold / Eric Marcus. -- First ed.
     p. cm.
     Includes index.
     ISBN 0-9720258-0-4
     LCCN 200209163

     1. Strategic Planning. 2. Creative Ability In Business. 3. Business Strategy 4. Leadership. 5. Organizational Change. 6. Management. 7. Electronic Commerce 8. Success in business 9. Information Technology Forecasting. 10. Information Technology Management. 11. Strategy, Corporate. I. Marcus, Eric   II. Title.

                         658.4'012-DC21

Strategies to Transform Your
Organization into Information Age Gold

THE DIGITAL
ALCHEMIST®

ERIC MARCUS

Mark,
To a truly inspiring
and forward-thinking Mark!
leader! Let's make
information age gold!

Eric

**STRATEGIC VISION
PRESS**

DEDICATION

To the Digital Alchemists® of today and tomorrow who come to work each day tirelessly working to create and sustain change in their respective organizations and to a person who has never known any boundaries and has always made me the proudest father in the world, my daughter Elizabeth.

Acknowledgements

I would especially like to thank my many clients including Jennifer Allerton (Roche Pharmaceuticals), Bob Crawford (Brook Furniture Rental), Mark Miller (Cendant), Nancy Wilson Smith (National Association of Realtors®), Mark Wilberts (Land O Lakes), Carl Wilson (Marriott International), Mahvash Yazdi (Edison International), and Heidi Youngkin (Johnson & Johnson), as well as my thought partners including Susan Annunzio, Judith Kohn, Wendell Cox, Charles Perrottet, Terry Rooney, Christina Rice, Vonda Shannon, James Ware, and Etta Weinstein Marcus for helping me develop and practice the art of Digital Alchemy®. I would also like to expressly thank Peter Cochrane for his ongoing support and friendship including writing the Foreword to this book. I would like to thank my father, Mel Marcus, for always challenging me and for being a role model of honesty, integrity, and honor. Thanks to Brian Taylor, Michael Morris, and Nina Taylor for their remarkable editorial and design contributions, which have made *The Digital Alchemist*® come alive.

DIGITAL ALCHEMY®

(dij'e-tel al'ke'me) n., 1. A pattern-breaking way of thinking aimed at radically increasing value by highly leveraging knowledge and intellectual capital. 2. The process by which an organization is transformed for success in the digital age.

ABOUT THE ALCHEMY GLYPHS

Throughout this book, at the start of each Strategy, you will find symbols known as alchemist's glyphs. These glyphs were used by ancient alchemists to symbolize various substances and processes. Just as alchemy has been associated with the idea of transmutation, or the fundamental change of one thing into another, Digital Alchemy® employs the tools developed by Corporate Alchemy, Inc. to help companies transform their industrial-age businesses into tomorrow's information age leaders. All the glyphs used throughout this book carry the meaning of gold, except for the first one below, which means air, and was used for its visual appeal.

TABLE OF CONTENTS

Fast-Foreword. xxi
Introduction xxv

SECTION ONE: Introduction to Digital Transformation 1

Digital Transformation: What's Going On? 3
About Digital Alchemy®. 13
Digital Alchemy® Process. 17
Attributes of a Digital Alchemist® 23
What Is Your Digital Alchemist® Aptitude? 24

SECTION TWO: The Digital Alchemy® Process 29

The Digital Alchemy® Process: Understand 31
000001 (1)   The Critical Drivers of Technology-enabled
                    Business Strategy. 33
000010 (2)   Information Transparency and
                    Ruthless Darwinism 36
000011 (3)   Reassessing What Business You Are In 38
000100 (4)   Understand Cyberpsychographics. 41
000101 (5)   Identify Your Micromarket Segmentation 45
000110 (6)   Benefit From One-stop Shopping
                    Customer Convenience. 49
000111 (7)   Welcome to E-communities 51
001000 (8)   Turn the Web into a Fast Feedback
                    Customer Party Line. 53
001001 (9)   Decide Whether to Niche or Consolidate 56
011100 (10) Glocalize 59
001011 (11) Accelerate Technology Adoption Naturally. 61

The Digital Alchemy® Process: Innovate 65
001100 (12) Anticipating Change And Proactively
                    Innovating Strategy. 68

001101 (13) Leverage Anywhere, Anytime
Wireless Communications 74
001110 (14) Profit from Invisibly Embedded Intelligence 76
001111 (15) Leverage Information about Information 79
011000 (16) Create Personalized Customer Experiences 81
010001 (17) There Ain't No Such Thing as a "Web Page" 83
010010 (18) The Internet Is Changing Advertising from
Active to Passive 85
010011 (19) Add a New Dimension to Your Sales
and Marketing Initiatives 88
010100 (20) Learn to Write for Machines. 90
010101 (21) Put Software Agents to Work. 94
010110 (22) Extend Your Brand into Cyberspace. 96
010111 (23) Productizing and Servicizing:
Ernie and the Pacemakers 99
011000 (24) Collaborative Systems: Be Here, Be There
and Be Effective 101

The Digital Alchemy® Process: Align 107
011001 (25) Different Carrots Drive New Behaviors. 109
011010 (26) Agility: The Most Critical Skill of
the Information Age 112
011011 (27) Knowledge Management Accelerates 118
the Learning Curve
011100 (28) Create New Roles in Your Organization 120
011101 (29) Develop Your Own Digiprise®. 123
011110 (30) Wire Up Collaborative Value Networks 126

The Digital Alchemy® Process: Deliver. 133
011111 (31) Drive One-on-One Customer
Relationship Management 135
100000 (32) Create Effective Knowledge Repositories
Intranets and Villages 149
100001 (33) Buy, Pay, and Price in Real Time 142
100010 (34) Participate in the Internet Digital Marketplace. . . 147

Table of Contents

100011 (35) Measure Your Information Age Value (GKP) . . . 150
100100 (36) Take Advantage of
Interactive Technotainment 153

The Digital Alchemy® Process: Going Forward. 157

SECTION THREE: Appendices 161

Resources and Tools 163
Appendix 1: Web Sites of Interest to Digital Alchemists®. 165
Appendix 2: Glossary 171
Appendix 3: Index 177
About the Author. 193

LIST OF FIGURES

Figure   1:   Will Competition In The 21st Century in
                Your Industry Look Like It Does Today?. 8
Figure   2:   Your Business Strategy Should Effectively
                Leverage Digital Age Techniques 11
Figure   3:   About Digital Alchemy®. 15
Figure   4:   The Digital Alchemy® Process 18
Figure   5:   Reassessing What Business You Are In 39
Figure   6:   How Does Your Business Strategy Address
                Channel Management and Your Channel Roles?. . . 66
Figure   7:   New Supercompetitor Target (Your Business). . . . 69
Figure   8:   The Innovation Pyramid 70
Figure   9:   SAGE: Managing in Uncertain Times. 72
Figure   10:   Broadband, Wireless, and Internet 2 75
Figure   11:   Embedded Computing 77
Figure   12   The Advent of Personalization 82
Figure   13:   Add a New Dimension to Sales and Marketing. . . 89
Figure   14:   Content Management. 92
Figure   15:   Be Brand Intensive, Not Capital Intensive 97
Figure   16:   The Digiprise®: A Collaborative Value Network . 104
Figure   17:   The Future of The Digiprise® 130
Figure   18:   One-on-One Customer
                Relationship Management 138

LIST OF TABLES

Table 1: Transformational Characterizations
           and Limitations 5
Table 2: Technology-enabled Business Strategy 34
Table 3: Shifts in Customer Expectations. 44
Table 4: Supercompetitor Template 79
Table 5: XML. 91
Table 6: Agents 95
Table 7: Examples of B2B Digital Marketplaces. 148
Table 8: Industrial vs. Digital-age Values. 152

Fast-Foreword
By Peter Cochrane

Mr. Cochrane was head of research for British Telecommunications from 1993-1999 and in 1999 he was appointed Chief Technologist. In November 2000, Peter retired from BT to join his own startup company — ConceptLabs — which he founded with a group out of Apple Computers in 1998. A graduate of Trent Polytechnic and Essex University, he was the Collier Chair for the Public Understanding of Science & Technology at the University of Bristol from 1999 to 2000. He has published and lectured widely on technology and the implications of information technology. His numerous awards include an Order of the British Empire (OBE) in 1999 for his contribution to international communications, the IEEE Millennium Medal in 2000, and The City & Guilds Prince Philip Medal in 2001.

Is there any science in business and can we predict the economics of the future? I don't think so! In comparison to the physics, chemistry, and engineering that drive our global economy, business models and understanding seem to be in the dark ages — when all you needed to be a scientist was a pointy hat. Most business executives seem to talk of myth and legend, heroes and villains, rapid success and failure, of a world full of surprises and danger, that is not only inherently nonlinear and chaotic, but increasingly so. Mighty giants are slain by the apparently insignificant actions of lawyers and regulators, whilst tyrannical and unheeding managers take once powerful companies and drive them to ruin in months. And just now and again some accidental new industry or company is born that exhibits unbelievably rapid growth and completely changes the business, financial, and management landscape.

One vision of the alchemists is that of wizened old men in caves and cellars dedicating their lives to the conversion of lead into gold. But in reality these experimentalists gave birth to science and true understanding. They observed, they thought, they experimented and recorded, and progress was slowly made. As a direct result we now have methods, models, and rigor that are the hallmarks of the scientific process. But in business we are still at the stage of observing and experimenting, deciding on the right questions, and questioning the answers. And more often than not exclaiming, "How the heck did that happen!" It might be that a fully mature business science will never emerge, as our technologies continue to develop faster than our society. It might be that technological progress will surpass our limited and mainly linear thinking, enabling machines to try to make something of it all. But until that day comes we had better continue observing, recording, and rationalizing best we can, for the future wealth and well-being of the planet rests with our ability to understand — and understand fast.

There has never been a time like this! We can communicate and travel at will, and we can create business on the edge of technology. So many business books can tell you what has already happened, but so very few can give us a glimpse of what is to come and what should be done. I have known Eric Marcus for over a decade and worked with him on many projects. He has been a consummate observer and experimenter in the field of business, an alchemist bearing the cusp of change, leading those striving to change before it is too late. His portal to the leading edge has been as a consultant to some of the leading players across the planet. And in that role he has devised many frameworks, thought processes, and strategies to avoid the catastrophes awaiting those who do not heed the warning signs.

This then is Eric's book, his chart of experience and wisdom gained from being on the leading edge for over ten years — a time of transition from relative economic stability, to an eBoom, dot.com bust, the 9/11 NY shockwave, and the rapid economic recovery to near sanity. A period that saw the creation of the rust belt, the rise of the bit over the atom, mobile operators raped of $Bns by governments for near worthless 3G licenses, and the Enron debacle taking out Andersen. But from all this Eric distills his core themes, values, business life and blood as he charts the thinking and experience of a latter day alchemist.

This book is a primer for more than business survival. It is for everyone — white collar, blue collar, no collar, chairman, board member, manager, and staffer. It is far more holistic than most business books. Its historical and present day examples span steel production, energy supply, telecom and IT, working practices, creativity, and management. The British Gas example is an excellent study in corporate and government stupidity on a par with Enron in the U.S. I think the people involved in both should have read this book! I enjoyed and appreciated the links to Sun Zi's and the thirty-six strategies for success/victory, the self test questions, and the beyond "faster, better, cheaper" thinking.

In every aspect of my life I have sought out people of different backgrounds and disciplines to enrich and widen my thinking processes. I have also read widely, attended conferences and presentations, and looked to learn from any available source. I have no idea how you, the reader, think or strategize, but I can guarantee that you will do it in a different manner than me or anyone else. What I can guarantee is that you will find something in this book that will change the way you see and think of the world of technology and business. How can I give you such a guarantee? Because I have created and brought to market many new technologies and companies in the last decade, and here I found food for thought, new perspectives, and insights. And anyway — it is a good read!

Peter Cochrane
ConceptLabs CA Co-Founder
Somewhere over the North Atlantic
8th April 2002

Introduction

The *Digital Alchemist*® is designed primarily for those of you who lead traditional businesses. In all likelihood you have experienced success but now find the rules changing. Globalization, consolidation, nontraditional competitors, disruptive technologies, and other factors are challenging the way business is and will be done. Transforming today's businesses requires new ways of thinking. It is definitely challenging, but at the same time it offers enormous payoffs.

The *Digital Alchemist*® is a guidebook to strategically transforming your organization into information-age gold. It will help you anticipate trends as well as position your organization to take advantage of emerging developments. Its goal is nothing short of helping you change the fundamental rules of competition in your business.

This book is divided into two major sections. The first section, Digital Transformation, examines our migration from an agrarian economy to an industrial economy and the current emergence of a digital economy.

Just as the assembly line was the hallmark of the industrial age, the digital transformation is already demonstrating the power of leveraging knowledge, personalizing, developing new channels, and even rethinking the very institution of the corporation.

The Digital Transformation explores shifts in customer perceptions, values, and expectations. It also describes the attributes of a Digital Alchemist.®

The second section, The Digital Alchemy® Process, is divided into its four major steps.

Understand
Segmenting customers as tightly as possible, acquiring as much customer information as possible, mining that data, and scanning for technological breakthroughs.

Innovate
Creatively innovating strategic thinking to result in a compelling vision that can change the rules.

Align
Assessing and filling gaps, developing success metrics, and ensuring business outcomes match organizational objectives.

Deliver
Piloting and then deploying the strategies and Digital Alchemy,® practices that will deliver the desired business outcomes – measured against success factors.

Within each of the four steps, the book details the thirty-six specific strategies that can be used to transform your organization. These strategies are designed to produce business outcomes that will help you and your organization deal with the challenges of the twenty-first century. They are not only prescriptive but are also illustrated with best practice examples collected from years of research.

The Digital Transformation will enhance your knowledge of the current environment and emerging trends. As you read The Digital Alchemy® Process you will be able to select specific strategies to introduce in your organization. While each strategy offers important concepts to understand and master, as a change agent you will likely want to be selective about which strategies you decide to implement in your organization and over what period of time. No matter which strategy or strategies you select, it is critical to employ an effective change-management discipline.

The Digital Alchemist® is a book for strategists, not technologists. It is about doing business in new ways. The strategies developed in the book are born of the digital age. Enabled by information technology, they empower organizations to leverage knowledge, enhance communications and collaboration, speed time to market, encourage innovation, reduce costs, change organizational behavior, and manage culture change.

You have the opportunity of a lifetime in front of you. We are moving from an industrial age world of constrained resources (capital, people, physical plant, etc.) to a world of unlimited resources (intellectual capital, global networks, etc.) in which the victor is far more likely to be the most clever, not merely the richest or biggest.

Become a Digital Alchemist® and you can be one of the leaders of the digital revolution, developing technology-enabled business strategies that create jobs and improve the way we live, work, and play.

Section One
Digital Transformation

Digital Transformation:

WHAT'S GOING ON?

Dot.coms rising and crashing. Computers and the Internet are pervasive. Business and our very way of life seem to be transforming at a faster pace than ever before. It seems as if change is out of control and that's an uncomfortable feeling.

The purpose of this book is to help you better understand why and how the world around us is changing and to position you to take advantage of those changes. The process we will use to do this is called Digital Alchemy® and our goal is to turn you into a master Digital Alchemist® who can anticipate and be a catalyst for change.

Are you prepared to become an information age leader? How about your business? The world is on the threshold of a digital transformation that will lead to new products and services and radically different processes. Everything about how we determine value as well as how we live, work, and play is dramatically changing. We already see computers on most desktops and in more than half of all homes in the United States. Yet, the biggest effects lie ahead as computers become an unseen part of nearly everything we do — computer ubiquity.

Successful businesses are making their products "smart" to create unique value. Smart factories are using computers to replace many of the physical limitations of their shop-floor machines. Smart homes are managing energy usage and offering other convenient features. Smart appliances are handling routine tasks, such as adding just the right amount of bleach to the wash. Adding knowledge to ordinary products is creating new value for customers.

Individuals who want to thrive in this new, fast-paced world must also change and keep changing. It used to be enough to become an expert in a particular skill. But with technological advances continuing to accelerate, today's skills age rapidly. And, since no one can predict future needs, our ability to be agile and anticipate change is our most important skill. If you are driving down the street and a small child suddenly darts out in front of your car, you can only slam on the brakes and hope to stop in time. If you are scanning the road ahead and see children playing you can anticipate the possibilities and slow down; then, when the child darts out you have alternatives (e.g., stop, turn into a driveway). Thinking several moves ahead pays off.

The information age changed the way I wrote this book. On one level it changed my writing style. While I have written for many

Table 1: Transformational Characterizations and Limitations

Economy	Characterization	Limitation
Agrarian	Farming, individual craftsperson	Acreage, amount of work a single person could do
Industrial	Asset-based, centralized, product-oriented, command & control, hierarchical, economies of scale	Physical constraints on resource capabilities and management (e.g., people, machines)
Information	Intellectual capital, blurred products and services, relationships	Organizationwide knowledge

years, I wondered how I would go about writing a book that would broadly appeal to those interested in improving their awareness of the enormous changes beginning to occur in the way we work. How would I develop a writing style that would motivate action? I took my own advice and did my writing on a smart pad of paper, namely Microsoft Word. But, I did more than just use it as a word processor. I used its grammar checker, thesaurus, and Flesch readability tests to improve my writing skills, suggest alternative sentence structures, and make better word choices. Technology amplified my abilities, leaving me more time to focus on the content I wanted to share.

Dematerialization

For roughly the last hundred years, we built an industrial economy. Immediately prior to that, we relied on an agrarian economy. Now we are transitioning into an information economy. Their respective characterizations and limitations are in Table 1.

In the agrarian age, a farmer's earning power depended on the amount of acreage, weather conditions, and the number of workers. A craftsman's earning power depended on the amount of work one person could do in a single day. Through centralizing, specializing, and taking advantage of economies of scale, the industrial age increased our earning power. Yet, while factories produced more goods, their output was still limited by physical constraints.

The information age is rapidly changing all of that.

Products and services are becoming commodities as consumers become more knowledgeable and networked. What this means is that the physical attributes of products and services, and even our business processes are becoming less and less important. In short, they are *dematerializing*. Automobiles are an excellent example. At one time, customers bought automobiles on the basis of physical appearance (color, lines, and even fins), or on the basis of a particular feature (cup holders, power seats), all of which have become "me-too" commodities. Today's automobile buyers, while still interested in these physical aspects, want much more. They want their automobiles to be smart. They want their automobiles to know where they are and navigate to where they're going. They want their automobiles to let them know when they need service. They want their automobiles to shift automatically into four-wheel or all-wheel drive and they want them to anticipate problems.

Physical limitations are also dematerializing our factories and plants as computer-driven machines increase the speed of production. For example, in one of its industrial age plants, Bethlehem Steel required three to four man-hours of labor to produce one ton of steel. By way of contrast, at the same point in time, Nucor Steel, through a knowledge-rich, computer-driven process, was making that same ton of steel in only forty-five man-minutes of labor.

In the future we will not be tied to the limitations of physical plants or machines that produce only a single part. We will see our businesses grow and succeed with dramatically reduced inventories, offices, and personnel.

More and more, we will scrutinize old notions of value. Intellectual capital such as know-how, experience, intuition, and shared learning are already becoming the main differentiators in our networked world. Knowledge and our ability to manage it will be our only constraints.

Digital Alchemists will play a key role in our transformation. They will put intelligence into products, services, and business processes. They will reduce cycle times and personalize their offerings. In fact, the way they deal with dematerialization will be the single greatest factor in determining their organizations' success in the information age.

Dematerialization is the increased focus on knowledge and intellectual capital, rather than merely physical capital and size, to create value. In the information age, dematerialization and the expectation of both rapid obsolescence and change is accelerating the acceptance of new technologies. Historically, it has taken between twenty and forty years to embrace a new technology and to truly understand its full impact.

Electric power is an excellent example of this slow adaptation. Edison built the first power plant in 1882, but by 1899 only 3 percent of U.S. factories used electric motor-driven machinery. Two decades later, only 33 percent of U.S. factories had shifted to electric power. Only by 1929 had a slim majority motorized. We lived in a much less competitive world and we had little expectation of major change.

Information age competition is compelling us to radically reduce the twenty to forty year gaps. Today there is less margin for error than ever before due to global competition and the accelerating rate of technology acceptance. The telephone, for example, took thirty-eight years to reach its ten millionth customer, while the cellular phone took only nine years to reach the same mark. The fax machine took twenty-two years, while the personal computer took seven, and the World Wide Web only two.

Unfortunately, many people and businesses only think about new technology as a way of incrementally improving existing products, services, and processes. They are simply making them faster, better, and cheaper. They frequently fail to reexamine themselves in light of new, technology-enabled business strategies. As a result, they make themselves vulnerable to new market entrants that are not constrained by old business methods. Further complicating things, with change coming so fast, it is nearly impossible for decision-makers to stay current on all of the latest business practices.

But speed of innovation is critical.

Will Competition In The 21st Century In Your Industry
Look Like It Does Today?

ASPs Competitors? **Value** **Channels**
Platforms? **Migration** Pricing and Price Discovery
Purchasing **Patterns?** Pricing and **eHubs**
Demand Aggregators Disintermediation?

Figure 1

Without the physical limits of the past, competitors have much lower barriers to entry and urgent action is imperative. To achieve market dominance and avoid being blindsided by new, innovative competitors, or to simply stay in business, we must change the way we do business now.

Redefining businesses

The information age transformation is forcing businesses to redefine themselves or be redefined by their competitors. Firms will compete less on the basis of products and more on the basis of business models — models that will change very quickly.

The energy industry illustrates this point. For years, energy companies operated in a regulated world. They didn't worry about competitors entering their protected territories. Today, they are being deregulated globally and forced to compete. They could simply cut prices but that is not a long-term strategy. Other businesses compete by making better mousetraps, but how does an energy company do that when its product (e.g., electrons) is a commodity, identical to that of its competitors?

To answer that question, we need to understand the changing nature of the energy business. Industry leaders are recognizing that their customers do not buy electrons or kilowatt-hours. Instead, they buy warm homes and offices, light, and heat for cooking. By wrapping their electrons with intellectual capital and knowledge assets, energy companies can create the "smarter electron." This new, value-added product will be able to deliver a whole new range of products. We will see the delivery of seventy-two degree homes and offices. Customers will be able to select levels of power (e.g., prime time, uninterruptible power). One-stop-shopping for all energy, telephone, Internet, and cable services (leveraging current customer service, billing, and engineering capabilities) will be the norm. The entire industry will change. Energy companies that just continue to sell electrons will go out of business.

Information age competition raises a new threat by also placing a premium on knowledge and intellectual capital. In fact, a digital competitor may only *be* virtual. For example, the law requires British Gas to carry anyone's gas over its transmission lines. A clever startup business, with no gas reserves, research and development expenses, or physical assets, could be formed. They could buy quantities of gas from British Gas (or any supplier) large enough to earn a discount. They could then sell this gas to British Gas's customers at a price between their cost and what the customer had been paying British Gas. Further, they could then require British Gas to deliver the gas to the customers (formerly British Gas's customers) over their transmission lines. This is simply one example of how a "green field" business with no physical assets can become a global competitor.

The information age has already impacted stockbrokers in a big way. Today, the same trade can cost $384 when executed by a full-service broker, $146 when executed by a discount broker, and only $8 when executed on the Internet through a brokerage such as Ameritrade. Does this predict the demise of the full-service broker? Probably not. However, consumers will use full-service stockbrokers only when those brokers add sufficient customer value to justify the additional expense.

Stockbrokers who just place trades are simply *information intermediaries*. They provide their customer access to the exchange. In the same way, real estate agents provide access to the multiple listing service, connecting potential buyers and sellers. However, the Internet is already stepping into this role. This means that stockbrokers, real estate agents, distributors, and many others must find new ways of adding customer value. This value may take the form of lowered costs, time savings, convenience, marketing expertise, knowledge of financing, or access to networks of third party providers.

Economies of Knowledge

Digital Alchemists® need to consider economies of knowledge rather than economies of scale. Economies of scale were a major driver of industrial age success. They reduced redundant costs by sharing services whenever possible. As a result, we saw the centralization of many business functions. However, companies such as British Petroleum have now found that while economies of scale result in short-term cost savings they also disperse accountability. Since the information age has dramatically reduced the costs of many of the previously centralized services, they have chosen to redistribute many of them to business units that now are fully accountable for their business outcomes. They need to understand that new values come into play in an economy in which intellectual property and relationships are the dominant components.

Let's look at an insurance company that wants to redefine itself for the information age. It needs to bypass industrial age thinking where economies of scale have produced only minor value, such as centers of business process outsourcing (e.g., claims, underwriting) that operate at high volumes but with low profit margins. Applying economies of knowledge, the company could develop whole new concepts of risk management, such as a digital insurance policy that uses sensors to monitor equipment performance on the shop floor. The policy price could be an agreed-upon formula that applies the data collected by these sensors rather than a fixed price.

The information age requires new models of thinking. Applying information technology to our own lives and to our organizations compels us to revisit our goals and objectives, look at the new capabilities we have been given, and then innovate. We need to rise to new challenges in the acquisition, representation, sharing, and manage-

Your Business Strategy Should Effectively Leverage Digital Age Techniques

Digiprise:®
Supplier through Customer
Connectivity and Collaboration

Dematerialization:
Leveraging Knowledge

New Channels:
Development and Conflict
Resolution Management

Personalization:
Markets of One

Dynamic Business Models:
Continuous Reinvention

Digital Assets:
Creating New Value

Web Time:
Ready-Fire-Steer

Infonomics & Variable Pricing:
e-conomics & Market Pricing

Figure 2

ment of intellectual capital and knowledge. They include collaborating and networking, using emerging information technology to go beyond "faster, better and cheaper" incremental improvements, and making the cultural and organizational changes needed to make it all work.

Digital Alchemy® enables us to creatively rise to these challenges, preparing our minds for new ways of thinking, envisioning the possibilities that will lead to entirely new approaches to excellence, exercising (and even enjoying) radical change, and ultimately rewriting the rules of competition in our industries.

But where can the practitioners of Digital Alchemy be found? The answer is: anywhere.

Working as a Digital Alchemist® requires spirit, heart, mind, openness, and energy. It demands the ability to think about information technology in a way that permeates every aspect of our lives. The Digital Alchemist® profile not only foreshadows a new corporate job description for the individuals responsible for understanding, recommending, and integrating emerging technologies, it calls upon us to transform the way we live our lives in much the same way as we did more than a century ago when we moved off the farm and into the cities and finally suburbs. The most successful individuals will learn to think like Digital Alchemists® on a continuing basis and organizations will encourage their top decision-makers to do likewise.

The digital transformation offers pain and gain. To those who embrace change rather than fighting the trends and technologies driving us into the next millennium, there will be opportunities for breakthroughs and profit. Some will thrive and others will fail. To those who close their eyes and hope this will all pass, there will be no opportunities for success. While we can look back and see the incredible changes brought by the twentieth Century, the digital transformation and elimination of many of the physical constraints of the industrial age will make them look quaint. You have the opportunity to make yourself and your organization an information age leader. The choice is yours.

Look for opportunities to expose and disintermediate non-value-adders.

About
Digital Alchemy®

More than ever, as individuals, managers, investors, and customers, we are recognizing the need to develop a vision of how the business landscape will change in a future that seems to be rapidly rushing toward us. But just as strategic objectives outlined by generals at war must be translated down to more specific tactics for field commanders, we must also be able to describe dozens of digital practices for taking action in the present.

However, digital thinking does not come naturally. To that end this book describes the "Thirty-six Digital Alchemy® Strategies" — techniques illustrated through vignettes of successful digital innovation, extended through Digital Alchemist® thinking, to foresee the future implications of powerful information age trends. Each strategy suggests a rather focused but powerful way to rethink your business and seize opportunities.

"The only new thing in the world is the history you don't know," said former U.S. President Harry S. Truman. And it is with a look to history that I chose to include thirty-six strategies in this book. A unique collection of ancient Chinese proverbs describing some of the most cunning and subtle strategies ever devised was called "Thirty-six Strategies." Other Chinese military texts such as Sun Zi's *The Art of War* focus on military organization, leadership, and battlefield tactics. The Thirty-six Strategies apply more suitably to the fields of politics, diplomacy, and espionage. These proverbs describe not only battlefield strategies, but also far more expansive tactics, such as the proverbs: "hide the dagger behind a smile," "kill with a borrowed sword," and "toss out a brick to attract jade." The origins of the Thirty-six Strategies are unknown. No author or compiler has ever been mentioned, and no date as to when it may have been written has been ascertained. The first historical mention of the Thirty-six Strategies dates back to the Southern Chi dynasty (AD 489-537) where it is mentioned in the Nan Chi Shi (history of the southern Chi Dynasty). By selecting the most important thirty-six strategies, this book honors this ancient Chinese text — perhaps one of the first books on business strategy ever written.

The Thirty-six Digital Alchemy® Strategies are grouped into the four steps of the Digital Alchemy® process: understand, innovate, align, and deliver. The strategies encompass:

- **Infonomics** — the business issues relevant to the Internet and the New Economy, including online purchasing, unique measurements of success in a digital world, auctions, and digital cash
- **TechKNOWvation** — the strategic business implications of emerging technologies, including productization, servicization, informing, ubiquitous computing, the leveraging of information, and the new products and services we can anticipate
- **Cyberpsychographics** — the expectations, desires, wants, and needs of the digital customer

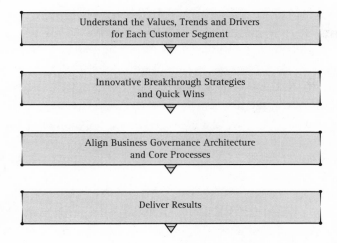

Figure 3

- **IntelliMarketing** — technology-enabled marketing strategies
- **Digiprise®** — the impact of the information age on the enterprise, including reward and recognition systems, new jobs and roles for the individual, and new forms of organization

Throughout this book you should be actively involved in the content. A Digital Alchemist® aptitude profile appears at the end of chapter one. At the close of each subsequent chapter you will be refocused through a set of action stimulators, challenging your mastery of specific Digital Alchemy® practices.

The transformation from an industrial to an information society is every bit as significant and far reaching as the transformation from the agrarian to the industrial age. To make the transformation, business executives, entrepreneurs, and small-business owners alike must become Digital Alchemists® to thrive in the information age. As the alchemists of old tried to transmute base metals into gold, today's Digital Alchemists® must transmute their industrial age businesses into digital age market leaders. They must recognize the attributes of successful information age people and organizations and identify the skills and attributes needed for them to share in that success. This book is a guide offering practical advice and tactics to the Digital Alchemists® who choose to take on this challenge.

Alchemists of old sought to do more than change base metals to gold. They sought to *perfect* them into gold. Digital Alchemists® do similarly as they work to perfect their organizations toward an information age metamorphosis. We will now consider the overall path the Digital Alchemist® takes to achieve this perfection. Throughout this process, the Digital Alchemist® creatively and insightfully works closely with an integrated team of business and technology professionals and must be unequivocally supported and sponsored by the chief executive officer.

Most importantly, the Digital Alchemist® must focus on the customer, customer, customer. As one who has reviewed countless business and e-business strategic plans, I can unequivocally say that even today, the single biggest problem I have with them is that their authors are inward-out focused (what can we do rather than what do our customers value). The Digital Alchemist® must not only be pragmatic, he must see his organization through the eyes of his customers — segment by segment, product by product, and service by service.

Think strategically about information technology

Digital Alchemy®
Process

Digital Alchemy® is a four-step process customized to meet the specifics of each fact setting. It begins with Understand and moves through Innovate, Align, and Deliver. There is also a feedback loop between the Understand, Innovate, and Align steps to enable new discoveries to enhance the effort. Then, the cycle begins again as new capabilities and market needs lead to further innovation.

Understand
Goal: Position yourself to best anticipate the future.
- Determine customer segmentation in detail within cost effectiveness constraints
- Acquire and represent data and information for all customers
- Apply tools, such as neural networks and data-mining soft-

The Digital Alchemy Process

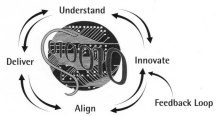

Figure 4

ware, to analyze and draw knowledge from all customer data by segment

- Understand values, trends, patterns, and drivers for each customer segment
- Understand your organization's goals, objectives, and strategies (including relationships and core competencies)
- Scan for technologies and technology-enabled products and services
- Focus on information age dematerialization to free the mind of industrial age constraints
- Become adept at understanding what technology can enable your organization to do (including using sources such as research and advisory services, competitive and market intelligence, academic institutions and technology innovators)
- Prepare to become a catalyst for change

The Digital Alchemist® can begin by looking at economic, technological, socio-political, demographic, and psychographic trends with an eye toward market directions. Then, match your forecasts against your personal interests, recognizing that work and play are merging in the information age. While this may seem daunting, it can be done easily by anyone willing to commit the time. A good starting place is to access the wealth of freely available information on the Internet (the Appendix contains a list of good web sites to start you off). Read magazines such as *Fortune*,

Business Week, and *Wired* and review other information that will keep you abreast of changes, breakthroughs, and potential marketplace disruptions.

Innovate:
Goal: Creatively innovate breakthrough thinking resulting in a compelling vision that can change the rules of the game in your industry and your life.

- Envision new technology-enabled practices that will accelerate the achievement of your organization's goals
- Identify business opportunities and needs (consider customers, shareholders, and employees)
- Envision cross-industry, cross-functionally, and in metaphor (processes, structures, systems, and culture)
- Invent ways of thinking differently — "How many different ways can I look at this?" as opposed to "Based on past experience, what is the best approach to take?"
- Go beyond verbal expression — draw, diagram, experiment, and so forth
- Think nonlinearly
- Innovate breakthrough new product, service, business process, and organizational development strategies
- State the innovation in terms of a compelling business vision (use feedback loop, as needed)

Digital Alchemists® become intensely and personally involved in perfecting change. They goes well beyond the "hows" to gain an in-depth understanding of the "whys." Asking fundamental questions that focus on the delivery of unique value, Digital Alchemists® challenge the essentials of viability in the information age.

Digital Alchemists® are highly valued for their insight. They have the ability to apply multiple perspectives and are visionaries. They are not restricted to linear thinking (i.e., going from point A to B to C to D) but are able to use newly available technology-enabled strategies to leapfrog from point A to D. Frequently they find that a solution is not obvious, yet can be found in other industries, functions, and concepts through metaphor, allegory, and analogy. For example, after working in the retail grocery store business, Charles Merrill returned to his beginnings on Wall Street. Analogizing the brokerage house to the grocery store he targeted the small investor, advertised, offered free services, and so forth to build a successful brokerage that continues to this day.

If you are beginning to practice Digital Alchemy®, you should begin by focusing on thinking in new ways. Keeping in mind the macro trend data and personal goals identified in the first step, shed preconceived notions and envision a future with as much imagination as possible. Mind expanding activities, such as brainstorming, meditation, and lateral thinking can be especially beneficial. Look at what you do best, what you enjoy doing, and what will be marketable. This may well result in the creation of whole new business models and invention of new jobs and roles.

Align

Goal: Evaluate gaps and any other needs required for implementation of the vision.

- Evaluate the organizational development and cultural issues involved in bringing the innovative vision to reality (e.g., what new behaviors will be required and what will motivate them?)
- Assess any existing business or technical gaps and determine how to transition to the desired state
- Develop supporting management structures and identify appropriate success metrics
- Use feedback loop, as needed

The Digital Alchemist® needs to develop a transition plan and governance structure that will provide the necessary infrastructure and support requirements as well as fill any gaps to bring the organization's vision to reality. This may involve business process changes, technological changes, and new reward and recognition systems.

Deliver

Goal: Develop the strategies and Digital Alchemy® practices and deliver the desired business outcomes.

- Innovate and try out alternative approaches for implementing the new vision
- Obtain business buy-in on the vision – be persuasive!
- Assist the business in prioritizing projects that lead to the vision
- Work with the business to select a small team to begin work
- Determine applicable Digital Alchemy® practices
- Test, evaluate, and correct digital practices in a controlled environment to achieve the desired vision (use feedback loop, as needed) – in no more than 90 - 120 days
- Develop and update a three-year forecast of the business impact of the Digital Alchemy® practices; consider all plausible alternatives (scenario planning and destroy-your-business workshops can be extremely effective)
- Implement the applicable Digital Alchemy® practices
- Monitor progress against your success metrics
- Make strategic adjustments, as needed

Digital Alchemists® recognize that they must make things happen. This is the step in which their crystallized vision is transmuted into a new practice in a controlled environment and tested prior to implementation. The Digital Alchemist® recognizes that time is of the essence and moves at Web speed. Market demands change so quickly that results must be produced in a short period of time to increase the likelihood of success. This means that big projects may have to be divided into smaller ones, but each must deliver measurable value.

There is no time for Digital Alchemists® to rest on their laurels. In our dematerialized world, the competitor who lags far behind cannot be underestimated. With their own Digital Alchemy®, they may well redefine the rules of competition in your business. The Digital Alchemist® must be constantly open to preparing anew as the cycle of continuous change keeps the quest for perfection alive.

Attributes of a Digital Alchemist®

Digital Alchemists® possess a unique blend of skills. They need to understand what technology makes possible yet they do not need to be technologists. They need to understand the organization and its strategic intent yet they do not have to be strategists, marketers, or business executives. To strategically apply digital practices, they must revisit the organization's mission and objectives, look at the new capabilities that information technology has enabled, and create ways to leapfrog over competitors with innovative products and services along with whole new ways of doing business.

This makes it critical for chief executive officers to recognize that the Digital Alchemist® must be far more than just the facilitator of yesterday's automation function. The Digital Alchemist® must have a place at the corporate strategy table and Digital Alchemy® must be seen as a strategic, competitive weapon. Look for broad-minded, Renaissance thinkers who can comfortably live at the ambiguous nexus of strategy, marketing, vision, practicality, technology, and business purpose.

MASTERING DIGITAL ALCHEMY®

What Is Your Digital Alchemist® Aptitude?
The following ten questions will help to evaluate your aptitude for digital alchemy. If you earn a high score, reading this book will expand your horizons and offer specific digital practices that your organization can implement. If you do not score as high, reading this book will help you see your organization from new perspectives and lead you to thinking in an entirely new way.

Questions
1. How many hours per week do you spend on the Internet exclusive of e-mail?
2. Can you name six information technologies that could accelerate the attainment of your organization's business goals?
3. Do you routinely print e-mail messages?
4. Can you view your organization from at least six different stakeholder perspectives (e.g., large customer)?
5. Do you communicate effectively with senior business management about technology implications and with technologists regarding business issues
6. How many different jobs (whether or not in the same organization) have you had in the last ten years?
7. What types of publications (in any media) do you read on a regular basis?
8. Do you believe information should be open or proprietary for

long-term organizational benefit?

9. What percentage of business transformation is directly related to people (e.g., change management, communications, etc.) vs. technology?

10. How many different industries have you worked in?

Scoring

1. 1 point if > 5; 3 points if > 8; 5 points if > 12
2. 1/2 point for each Yes (up to 6); 0 points for No
3. 2 points for No; 0 points for Yes
4. 1/2 point for each Yes (up to 6); 0 points for No
5. 2 points for Yes; 0 points for No
6. 3 points > 4; 2 points = 2 - 4; 1 point = 2; 0 points < 2
7. 1 point for each type: trade journals, technology publications, or business publications; extra point if any of the publications are received online — maximum of 4 points on this question
8. 0 points for proprietary; 2 points for open
9. 3 points > 94%; 2 points >89%; 0 points for other
10. 3 points > 5; 2 points = 3 - 5; 0 points for < 3

The Results

- High Aptitude: 23+
  You are already on your way to becoming a Digital Alchemist®. This book will hone your skills in specific Digital Alchemy® practices and offer you new perspectives.
- Moderate Aptitude: 14 – 22
  You have the basic skill set to be a Digital Alchemist and are about to learn to think about your organization and the competition in a whole new way.
- Low Aptitude: 0 – 13
  Much of what you are about to read will probably be new. Reading this book will open new doorways and show you new ways to compete in the information age.

As Digital Alchemy® is truly an art, I sincerely welcome comments and criticisms from all readers. Comments may be e-mailed to the author at ekmarcus@corporatealchemy.com or sent from our web-site: www.corporatealchemy.com.

Section Two
The Digital Alchemy® Process

The Digital Alchemy® Process:

UNDERSTAND

As industrial age business models disappear, information age models are rising to replace them. These evolving models will reflect new sources of value and offer opportunities to exploit undervalued assets. There will be new ways to leverage interactive media, innovative pricing strategies, and new approaches to value existing assets that focus on the impacts of de-materialization. The Digital Alchemist® will seek out highly flexible ways of doing business that are capable of both centralized and decentralized simultaneous operations.

The information age offers a whole new way of interacting with customers and carries with it a new set of responsibilities. Using the Internet, consumers can request product information, place orders, make billing inquiries, and countless other customer service activities. Within a few years, the phenomenal growth in Web users will plateau. But by then, the people using the Net worldwide will number in the hundreds of millions — if not billions.

As this transition happens, we have to understand how the psychographics — the wants, desires, values, and habits of consumers — change as they enter cyberspace. In short, we have to comprehend a new notion that will hereafter be known as "cyberpsychographics." Further, we need to understand that the capability to do interactive marketing requires a fresh look at what is being marketed and how that process should be conducted with the new tools available to us. All of this must be integrated with the cyberpsychographics of the customer and the new techniques they will find most attractive.

Sample best practice companies include:
- Auto-By-Tel
- Marriott
- PriceLine
- First Direct (U.K.)
- Merck
- Starwave
- Lexus
- Presley Homes

1
000001

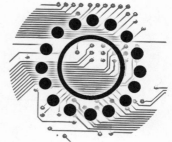

The Critical Drivers of Technology-enabled Business Strategy

Technology-enabled business strategies afford organizations the opportunity to create breakthrough value adds for their customers. Let's consider the business outcomes we can anticipate from just four critical technologies.

High-speed Computing
Ever faster, smaller processor chips are the cornerstone of many of the digital age's opportunities. They enable low cost telecommunications, smaller devices, and better human-machine interfaces (e.g., voice recognition and speech synthesization). Telephone-only call centers are being replaced with computer telephony interface (CTI) communications centers that let the customer decide how they want to do business with you (e.g., phone, fax, computer).

Table 2: Technology-enabled Business Strategy

Technology	Enabled Business Strategy
High-speed Computing	Driving down telecomm and processing costs, enabling cost centers to be profit centers
Broadband, Wireless, Narrowcasting, and Ubiquitous Computing	"Always On" connection to customers creates customer intimacy, and precision marketing
Data Mining	Understanding more about your customers to better price, bundle, select partners, and develop new products
eXtensible Markup Language (XML)	The Internet's *lingua franca* enabling real-time, seamless connectivity with legacy systems and Web personalization[1]

Broadband, Wireless, Narrowcasting and Ubiquitous Computing

Low cost, nearly infinite band wireless communications mean so much more than anywhere, anytime movies. It means having a tiny chip in your credit card that silently announces to the department store you've just entered that you've arrived. With the warehouse of data they have on your preferences and buying patterns, a personal concierge can be sent to assist "big spenders." Or as you walk down the street, a promotion for a Bach CD you've been wanting to buy can be directed right to you as you stroll within a block of the retailer. Tiny computers will be everywhere — sensing, assisting, broad- and narrowcasting. Privacy issues will also need to be addressed.

Data Mining

This is the process of identifying the habits of your customers through linear and neural techniques. What do they buy when they buy your products and services? From whom? What is your current customer wallet share? How quickly can you identify a change in these patterns and respond?

---

[1] "Lingua Franca" — an Italian phrase for "common language"

eXtensible Markup Language

This protocol enables legacy systems to be connected to Web sites, allowing real-time changes in one place to be systemically reflected. XML improves Web searches and navigation. Perhaps more importantly, it is the technology that will serve as the *lingua franca* of the Internet making it possible for every viewer to enjoy an individually unique experience – their own window on the Web.

Information Transparency and Ruthless Darwinism

Ubiquitous information flow at high speed and low cost has leveled the playing field between buyers and sellers and created even more competitive markets. In the past, sellers benefited from buyers' lack of knowledge, especially regarding pricing. However, today's buyer need only log onto the Web to do instantaneous price comparisons.

A major chemicals firm with operations around the globe found itself in a difficult situation. Its U.S. subsidiary created a comprehensive Web site – including pricing information. One day, the managing director of the firm's Australian subsidiary received a call from one of their largest and most long-term customers who said they were taking their business to someone else. Was it a service issue? No. Was it a quality issue? No. It seems that a purchasing staffer had been browsing the Internet and found the U.S. site. Even with duties, transport costs, and so forth, the U.S. prices were less expensive so they were going to buy from them. The U.S. organization was told to get their prices off of the Web page. However, in a competitive market, that's no answer. Competitors would have simply posted prices. Of course, what really ensued was a price-cutting war. It is not that your company cannot charge different prices in different parts of the world. Rather, it is that you must assume your customers can learn about your pricing practices and you must be able to justify the differentials to their satisfaction.

Electronic trading and information transparency has removed nearly all of the friction from today's financial markets. The Internet is already beginning to have the same impact on product/service markets and the talent market. Not too long ago, several smart, recent computer science graduates packaged themselves as a team and auctioned their services for a year on eBay.

Electronic markets have created global competition in nearly every industry

Reassessing What Business You Are In

It's not news that there's no money in making slide rules today. If slide rule manufacturers had understood the business impact of the semiconductor long before the first machine with "big green numbers and little rubber feet" became a reality, they would have been in a position to either transform their organizations or sell out while the going was good. Choosing to transform, a slide rule company could have become one of the early calculator – or even PC – makers. But how would semiconductors have even appeared on their radar screen? The slide rule company had to be able to redefine itself in the context of technologies that had the prospect of disrupting their markets. Defining themselves as slide rule manufacturers would lead them to use technology to improve their product and possibly increase short-term profits. Redefining themselves as manufacturers

Reassessing What Business You are In

Figure 5

of problem-solving devices — even mathematical problem-solving devices — would have taken them down a much more successful path.

Emerging information technologies are breaking down traditional barriers between industries and blindsiding many companies that don't realize they must reevaluate what it is they really do for a living. Let's use a restaurant guide publisher as an example. Rather than defining its work as publishing, it could redefine its work as the business of helping people find the right dining experiences. Instead of concentrating on making money by printing and distributing guides for $9.95 per copy, this company could then expand its horizons, finding a bigger growth opportunity in selling a wireless data service. When traveling anywhere in the world, a consumer could use a hand-held device to tap into the service to get a list of five of the best restaurants in that location — complete with a full review and directions.

Digital Alchemists® evaluate their businesses by looking at the way their customers use their products and services to create value. Major transformations such as we are now facing offer opportunities as well as threats. We are not flying on Union Pacific Air today because the railroads could not see beyond a very limited definition of their business.

Evaluate your business by looking at how your customers use your products and services to create value. How is your company integrated into their value proposition? Are there opportunities to

39

create more value? Can your current information assets be used to create new products and services? By answering these questions, you might find that you're not in the business you think you're in.

Understand Cyberpsychographics

Cyberpsychographics (the wants and desires of customers in an online world) are clearly different from the psychographics of the physical world. Customers are open to, and in fact pushing organizations toward, new ways of doing business and have shown strong interest in taking control of their own transactions from package tracking to ordering flowers. But there are also costs.

Our expectations change as we enter cyberspace. Just as you have different expectations when you enter Taco Bell versus when you enter a fine French restaurant, you have different expectations when you interact with a company in cyberspace versus one you interact with in the physical dimension.

Specifically, how do expectations change? When consumers could only transact business in a store or other physical location, they understood the reality that there would be times the business would be closed. On the Internet, customers expect you to be open 24 hours a day, 7 days a week, 365 days a year. When inquiries were sent by mail, consumers expected it to take a couple of days to get there, a day to be answered, and a couple of days to come back (at best!). Today, consumers expect instantaneous responses to their e-mail (within the day at worst case).

As cyberspace expands, customers will expect customized products and services. They will expect things to happen faster than ever before. They will come to expect their transactions to be fun. They will expect to enter a high-level dialog with other people. They won't simply read an advertisement; they'll expect to interact with it and place orders for the advertised product. And that's just the beginning. The cyberpsychographics of consumers will change in hundreds of subtle yet important ways. It is up to senior managers to make sure that their companies are not just reacting to new levels of expectations but actively setting those levels — in effect creating the cyberpsychographics for their industry.

How long do we have to make these changes? Begin preparing your business today for the video-game generation. PC shipments are beginning to surpass TV shipments and Coopers & Lybrand recently reported that 58 percent of Internet users indicated their online time comes at the expense of watching television. Soon, we are likely to see the average person spend more hours on the Internet than watching movies on their VCR. That hours-per-week figure tends to be even higher for the group of people who have grown up with the technology.

As online time cuts significantly into overall media time, especially among the young, companies need to adapt to new attitudes, habits, and mentalities that will soon be predominant. That means you must integrate information networks into every aspect of your relationship with consumers. And it means taking for granted that your potential customers will be immersed and well versed in the technology by the time they are working in the marketplace. They will expect to be able to buy your products and services online. They will expect instant gratification. They are starting with the PC and then looking at how you do business, not the other way around.

Already, the expectation levels of the video-game kids are spreading to other age groups. Hallmark and American Greetings have created kiosks where their customers can create their own cards. In so doing, they have demonstrated the importance of information over inventory and enabled their customer to personalize the end product. Kids are persuading their grandparents to get online so that they can swap e-mail. In fact, the fastest growing segment of the population now going online is the over-55 crowd, according to Nicholas Negroponte, founder of the MIT Media Lab. Still, the kids are weaving all this technology into the fabric of their lives, not just layering it on top like the older folks. Not only must CEOs prepare to sell products and services to this generation, but you also must prepare to hire them as employees.

Self-service is often the highest level of service that your company can provide. On a basic level, this is counterintuitive: Since when does a self-service buffet, for instance, make for better service than well-trained waiters? But for many products and services, consumers prefer to help themselves. Give a customer the means to do that and you have forged a strong bond with them. The overall goal is to provide 24-hour-per-day access to anything the customer needs.

A basic example of this is PeopleSoft, Inc., a leading provider of enterprise applications software. They operate a Web-based support service called the PeopleSoft Customer Connection. This self-service communication resource gives PeopleSoft customers and business partners 24/7 worldwide, online access to PeopleSoft product support, updates and fixes, PeopleSoft news and information, continuously updated documentation, and registration for training courses. "With Customer Connection, we've enhanced our industry-leading service offerings with a self-service information gateway," said the vice president of customer services for PeopleSoft. "Real-time access to critical information through the Internet eliminates time-consuming phone tag and enables PeopleSoft customers and

Table 3: Shifts in Customer Expectations

Shift	New Expectation
Things that Think	Doing Business Anywhere, Anytime
Frictionless Commerce	Accelerated Commoditization
Web Speed	Real-Time Management & Operations
Connectivity/Exchange Precision Marketing	Mass Customization
Low-Cost Communication	Interact Directly with End Customers and Build Community

business partners to search for information and resolve their issues at any time of day or night."

Banks are doing the same thing as they set up personalized computer telephony systems and Web sites. It has become commonplace to see online bill pay, account information, and transfer services.

Most importantly, these approaches to interfacing with customers shift control to the customer. The customer can decide when and the extent to which they choose to make contact. Federal Express was the pioneer in proving that customers themselves wanted this shift. When it introduced its online package tracking system and shifted control, as well as the cost of toll free numbers, computers, and customer service representatives, to its customers who responded with overwhelming approval.

Identify
Your Micromarket
Segmentation

Most companies are awash in data — data that could bring them closer to their customers and data that could lead them to develop more successful products and services. Yet most of them cannot find the data nuggets they need when they need it. In the future, those who can find information quickly and rapidly detect customer patterns will have a strategic advantage. They will be able to make more informed decisions, and they will be able to make them more quickly.

Data mining is the identification of valid, novel, potentially useful and ultimately understandable patterns in data that are not simply an extraction or aggregation of existing data. It begins by gathering every piece of information available about your customers — even data purchased from third parties such as MetroMail and R. L.

Polk — and then running state-of-the-art computer algorithms against that information to detect patterns that are frequently not discernable to the human eye.

Internet viewer "clickstreams" leave a trail that can be stored and mined (in addition to data acquired through on-site active registration). Data mining is more than just a single technique — it is a set of statistical methods used to identify data trends, patterns, and relationships. Data mining can create many different kinds of models; the two most popular are classification and clustering. In classification, profiles are created and data is mapped against them. In clustering, the data itself is used to create the patterns.

Data mining can be used to generate business outcomes such as:

- An analysis of customer acquisition and retention promotions over time
- Learning which combinations of what products and services are acquired by customers
- Identifying meaningful market segments using profile and Web activity data

Currently, there are at least forty companies providing data mining tools and the market for these products is just beginning to heat up. Most still have problems that must be overcome (e.g., not enough data-mining algorithms offered to provide a fully robust solution, insufficient database application programming interfaces, etc.), but we are likely to see these problems resolved in the next couple of years. Further, the increased use of data warehouse and On-Line Analytical Processing (OLAP) architectures and marketing-oriented user interfaces will accelerate this trend.

In the physical world, it may not be economically feasible to set up a shop in a particular area because there are simply not enough people in the community to support it. By applying data mining techniques, businesses in cyberspace can move beyond geographical limitations and "slice-and-dice" demographics and markets in ways never before thought possible.

One example is Starwave Corporation, a company that used on-line services to appeal to people's passions and interests. Their number one service was ESPNET Sports Zone, which was drawing more than three million hits a day. Unlike America Online or the Microsoft Network, which use breadth of coverage to attract subscribers, ESPNET vertically targeted people with a passion – sports. Other such vertical passions targeted by Starwave included Mr. Showbiz (entertainment gossip), Outside Online (outdoor enthusiasts), and Family Planet (parents). They were so successful, that Disney ultimately bought them out.

Rather than broadcasting to the masses and going for a high quantity of hits, Starwave narrowcasted for what they called *smart hits*. They spent time understanding the demographics of each of their services and they told advertisers they could deliver this specific, mini-mass-market to you (e.g., you can advertise in a specific content area at a specific time, pinpointing an audience that will be 96 percent male between the ages of eighteen and twenty-four).

Narrowcasting not only applies to advertisers, it also applies to content providers. The same approach could be used to target news, information, and other content to individuals or businesses.

Marriott Vacation Club International is one of the largest sellers and dealers of time-share condominiums. Their time-share condos allow people to buy a week or more of vacation per year for the rest of their lives. Time-share condos can also be swapped. If you want a change, you can trade your week in a Florida condo for a week in California, Hawaii, or even Europe.

In the past, Marriott marketed and sold condos through mass mailings to potential customers. This was a costly shotgun approach. Most mail went to people who were not interested. With the use of data mining software, Marriott is able to more clearly target potential customers. Data mining software allows Marriott to categorize and analyze names, usually from their hotel guests. Data from motor vehicle records, warranty cards, and property records can also be used. The data mining software takes this mountain of data and recognizes patterns and trends.

Marriott can also augment their database by purchasing third party data such as customer ages, number and ages of children, the cars they drive, hobbies, and even their estimated incomes. This data can then be analyzed to determine who is most likely to respond to a brochure advertising a time-share condo. The results? The response rate to Marriott's direct mailing program increased by more than 30 percent. Since each mailing costs about $1.50, the cost savings was dramatic. In addition, Marriott was able to reach customers that it may not have even tried without the data mining software.

But organizations must also be aware of growing consumer concerns about violations of their privacy. Cookies — programs that some Web sites download onto your hard disk to track your activities and similar monitors — are beginning to come under fire. The best solution for today is to make sure your customers know how you are using the data you collect about them and give them the opportunity to opt in or opt out at their own discretion.

Know more about your customers than your customers know about themselves.

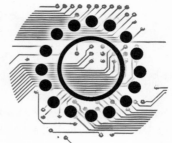

Benefit from One-Stop Shopping Customer Convenience

One of the problems with the Internet is its lack of convenience – it's still too hard to get things done. But that shortcoming can also be an opportunity. When customers are shopping online for products and services, they do not want to go to seventeen places to get what they want. They want timeliness and convenience. One-stop shopping is as powerful a selling point in cyberspace as it is in the physical world.

Let's look at Auto-By-Tel (www.autobytel.com) where a customer can research new and used car prices, check into financing options, purchase a new or used car, obtain financing, and get a quote on and purchase car insurance. Over one million customers have used this free service, which taps into a network of more than 2,700 dealers nationwide. Though sophisticated and much more convenient than having to go to all of those places on your own, this site still does not push the edge of what could be done.

Imagine going to a single Web site — let's call it the AutoAgent. A tranquil voice asks if the customer knows what kind of car he wants to buy — if not, it takes him through a series of questions that lead to that result. From there, the voice asks some questions relating to financing and insurance. Then, while AutoAgent is shopping for the best financing and insurance on the market, the customer is shown auto reviews in Consumer Reports, obtains a dealer invoice for the list of options he wants, gets a Kelly Blue Book price for his trade-in car, lists that used car on an exchange, buys a car, selects the best financing and insurance options, buys an extended warranty, and even, perhaps, joins an auto club.

What's the main difference between Auto-By-Tel and AutoAgent? Auto-By-Tel operates by linking to various sites. Yet, in cyberspace there are no physical locations, so why all that linking? AutoAgent would allow a customer to stay in one place and answer questions only once. AutoAgent does all of the work for me. The company that runs AutoAgent could be anyone who is able to forge the right relationships with various companies and agencies. Obviously the company's main goal would be to offer all these products and services together under one virtual roof. Any company that can integrate related transactions in this way will gain a critical edge when it comes to gaining the attention of buyers.

7
000111

Welcome to E-communities

Electronic communities offer organizations an opportunity to do good and to build or enhance customer relationships. E-communities are forums in which people are held together by a common affinity – a hobby, a career interest, a lifestyle, or a product. The community exists primarily for the enjoyment of its members and, while it may be sponsored by an organization, it usually develops its own personality, unlike a standard Web site.

These interest, or affinity, groups can convene around almost any topic. A group of creative writers from all around the U.S. may choose to meet in a cyberspace cafe every Tuesday at 9 p.m. Eastern Time. Occasionally they might invite a guest speaker. Anyone – groups of cardiologists, architects, chief information officers – can and do create their own electronic communities on the Internet. Many people participate in several electronic communities, developing and maintaining virtual relationships with people who they are unlikely to have met in the physical world due to geographic or other constraints.

Imagine you own a company that sells to seniors — perhaps you are a real estate broker specializing in the empty-nester market. By fostering a similar site you could provide a service to seniors and simultaneously keep the name of your business out front. You could also use the feedback gathered from the site to develop new products and services for seniors (or to provide to others, provided there was proper disclosure to the community and subsequent agreement). Then, consider that a community of interest could also be formed around any demographic, hobby group, profession or other group. The possibilities are unlimited.

8
001000

Turn the Web into a Fast Feedback Customer Party Line

Most businesspeople know that it is far less expensive to keep a customer than to acquire a new one. Consider this rule of thumb, cited by former Apple Computer CEO John Sculley: "If you lose a customer, not only do you lose that revenue, but it costs five times that lost revenue to finance the effort it takes to replace that customer. Looked at another way, it takes sixteen times the lost profits to replace him or her." Most businesses don't pay enough attention to this and have scant information about what customers want or how they feel about their products and services.

Feedback from customers should be ongoing. Your Web site can become a dynamic market focus group that tracks how visitors are responding to what they see, read, and hear. Let's use an automobile manufacturer as an example. You can determine not only how many people looked at your site but exactly what they looked at. If the data shows that most visitors are spending time learning about the safety features of your cars and that they are not at all interested in the specifications of the engine, then that can tell you a lot about how to build and market your cars in the future. And if you are able to obtain demographic information about those visitors, you can learn that certain features appeal to, say, women who are thirty-five to fifty years old.

Traditionally, companies have obtained this information via focus groups. Convening a focus group involves recruiting participants, bringing them together in one place, and paying them for their efforts. But now your Web site can collect this information for you 24/7 without the trouble of convening a group at all. The idea behind designing your Web site to also serve as an online focus group is to engage your customers in an interesting, ongoing dialog about how you can improve your products and services. You might even consider rewarding customers who take part by offering some token of value – it's a small price to pay for obtaining the competitive edge that comes from that information. What's more, doing it on the Web is much less expensive than convening a live group.

In many high-tech service industries, the cost of obtaining loyal customers takes on even more heightened importance. Consider AT&T's 1993 acquisition of McCaw Cellular. The telecommunications giant paid $17.5 billion for McCaw and its 2.3 million subscribers. That's more than $7,600 per subscriber. Clearly, AT&T should have done everything in its power to protect that investment. With so much competition in cellular service, these customers would cost way too much to lose and then replace.

The Internet, Value-Added Networks (e.g., America Online and Microsoft Network), and other digital media offer you the opportunity to dialogue with (rather than broadcast at) your customers twenty-four hours a day, seven days a week. They are essentially low-cost feedback loops in operation whenever and wherever your customers want to use them.

Companies including Charles Schwab, US West, Thomas Cook, Pfizer, Roxio, General Electric and many others use net.Genesis (www.net-gen.com/downloads/pdf/products/NetGenesis5_5.pdf), one of the many powerful Web site tracking and analysis programs to better understand customer behavior on their Web site, such as:

- Where visitors enter and exit the site (This information helps companies identify the most promising prospective customers)
- How frequently different software products are downloaded from their FTP site (This information guides development and marketing decisions)
- Exactly which organizations are using the FTP site (Sales staff can use this information as background material when calling on prospective customers)
- Which Web browsers visitors are using to access the site (This information allows site owners to build a picture of their Internet-savvy audience and determine whether or not to implement advanced technologies like JavaScript and frames)

Sales representatives can use this kind of software to view reports that correlate exactly to their geographic territories. They can also see what products each of their prospects has downloaded from the FTP site. This software can also closely integrate the sales process with the design of the company's Web site. With the insights provided by this kind of software, companies can refine elements of their Web sites to increase their effectiveness as a sales tool.

Most Web sites broadcast.
Look for ways to converse.

Decide
Whether to Niche
or Consolidate

To compete in the global marketplace, firms must have a certain critical mass of financial, technological, and human resources that are most easily offered by a large, multinational organization. However, for them to operate most efficiently, they cannot afford the luxury of investing in and servicing specialty or niche markets, requiring extremely high levels of customer intimacy and service.

As a result, the winners in today's marketplace are splitting into two tiers: the large, multinational players (including large alliances as well as nontraditional competitors looking to leverage their competencies in new marketplaces) and the small, niche players. The mid-size players are being squeezed out. It is critical to decide where you can and want to play in this developing market and select the appropriate strategies to make your organization successful. Companies are consolidating and forming alliances at faster and faster paces.

A senior pharmaceutical company marketing executive said, "All the mergers and acquisitions do make it seem that everyone wants to get bigger, whether for the right reasons or not. Actually, I think this trend opens up additional opportunities for companies such as ours, because as mergers make product lines grow, more companies will find that they really don't have the capability to promote what they would consider some of their smaller brands, which could well be large brands to companies like ours."

Then he said, "As I look at the market right now, I see three tiers of company sizes. There are the huge companies that have been getting bigger through mergers and acquisitions. Then you've got medium-sized companies that really aren't sure which way to go. They would like to be one of the big companies, but they're not big enough to be able to compete with the giants. At the same time they're too big to be successful as niche companies because they can't make decisions or move as quickly as we can. That leads me to conclude that all the consolidating of large companies that's going on adds to the role companies like ours can play and that the services we provide will be needed that much more. So I am confident that the niche companies will continue to grow in value."

The success of niche competitors such as Southwest Airlines, for example, challenges the common wisdom that only a few large international airlines will survive. Deep knowledge of a local or regional market and a cost structure appropriate to that market offer advantages against giants.

The real estate brokerage business is another example to consider. Prudential Florida (2600 agents) was sold to St. Joe Paper Co. for $90 million. Prudential had $3 billion in sales a year. St. Joe also owns Arvida Realty in Boca Raton (100 agents; $40 million in sales annually). The deal was almost all cash — $80 million cash, and $10 million paid over two years!

The impact of this kind of deal by a company outside the real estate brokerage industry is likely to result in a faster pace and increased accountability. A company with a lot of money to invest in technology and training will expect brokers and sales associates to increase productivity. Without technology savvy, you can't compete. They will be building expensive data warehouses and doing extensive data mining. They will also use the technology to measure performance.

There is also the expectation of instant results and accountability. The bottom-line will be scrutinized harder every quarter and performance will be expected to be high. There will be less time to develop people.

Consider that Cendant, the company that owns Avis and KFC, also owns real estate giants Century 21, Coldwell Banker, ERA, and PHH Mortgage. As it continues to grow, it will leave other franchisers and brokers to decide whether they can compete on a global basis or whether they should partner or secure a profitable niche today. Waiting too long to decide could be worse than making the wrong choice.

10
011100

Glocalize

A truly global business sees the world as its marketplace and:
- Solves client needs anywhere in the world
- Segments and personalizes global markets to reach individual customers
- Develops global products and services
- Encourages cultural diversity
- Reduces costs through access to less expensive resources
- Leverages economies of scale
- Increases operational flexibility
- Grows leaders who are
  - comfortable speaking multiple languages
  - willing to spend many years away from corporate headquarters

- flexible enough to manage the business in diverse parts of the world

At the same time we are seeing a strong shift to globalization, we are also seeing a strong shift to local control of local issues. Government and regulators in the middle are the ones who are giving ground.

This trend calls on businesses to *glocalize* — to simultaneously be global and local. Companies' efforts to be local often include a sincere sensitivity for issues such as the environment.

Comically, failures to glocalize are more often the case than the exception. Here are a few humorous examples.

- GM introduced the Chevrolet Nova in Mexico back in the 1970s. *No va* means "doesn't run" in Spanish.
- Pepsi's slogan "Come alive with the Pepsi Generation" meant "Pepsi will bring your ancestors back from the dead" in Chinese.
- In Chinese, the Kentucky Fried Chicken slogan "finger-lickin' good" meant "eat your fingers off."
- Parker Pen marketed a pen in Mexico and its ads were supposed to say: "It won't leak in your pocket and embarrass you." The company mistakenly thought the Spanish word *embarazar* meant "to embarrass." Instead the ads said: "It won't leak in your pocket and make you pregnant."

Accelerate Technology Adoption Naturally

To accelerate the widespread adoption of computers and the inclusion of technology in daily life we need more user-friendly interfaces. Communicating with computers should be as natural as communicating with a human being. The user interface of windows, icons, mice and pointers has kept many away from the benefits of the information age.

Consider the benefits of a speech-based interface:
- a more natural form of communication
- reaches beyond arm's length
- hands-free
- takes advantage of people having more "ear time" than "eye time"
- conveys important information through tone, stress, pitch, pause, and accent

- works with small objects, such as wristwatches or pocket devices
- would enable the blind, elderly, and people with arthritis or carpal-tunnel syndrome to use computers

Moore's Law, developed by Gordon Moore who went on to become the chairman of Intel Corporation, says that the capability of the microprocessor will double every eighteen months. More capacity means we can develop better interfaces. If we can expect least ten more iterations of Moore's Law, we can expect "instant on," speech recognition and synthesis, touchpad, 3-D, and even gesture-based (computer that can look at you and determine whether or not you need assistance) interfaces.

Virtual reality and other 3-D computer interfaces already offer improved interfaces. Virtual reality is helping companies reduce product development time, test new ideas, improve decision making, train employees, and revolutionize marketing. Today, with a Pentium processor, virtual reality software, and 3-D goggles, businesses can begin to experiment with simple virtual environments for less than ten thousand dollars.

Consider just a few of the applications of virtual reality. A major heavy equipment manufacturer has used a special room called a Cave Automatic Virtual Environment (CAVE) — a 3-D environment achieved by projecting 3-D computer graphics on display screens that surround the user. They model global operating environments and perform engineering work. In at least one situation they have reduced product development time from the expected five to seven years to three-and-a-half.

Virtual reality will greatly enhance marketing. Marketers will add virtual reality demonstrations to advertising as a way of introducing products to new customers. Focus groups will take on new importance in developing products when customers can actually try and respond to various options. Perhaps fashion designers, manufacturers, and buyers in different cities can use a CAVE to collaborate on new designs by entering a virtual catwalk. Virtual reality will also have widespread applications in training and education. An application already available from a company called World Builder allows trainees to tour a virtual factory to learn how to avoid health and safety hazards.

MASTERING DIGITAL ALCHEMY®

As a Digital Alchemist®, you should now be able to envision:

1. At least one asset of your organization that is not currently being used as a revenue-producing product and how it could become one
2. A new way of thinking about at least one aspect of your business that would create a competitive advantage
3. A way of valuing an intellectual property asset of your organization that is not currently being valued
4. How an aspect of your business could be better operated if managed in real time
5. A proactive approach to interactively marketing one of your products that goes beyond today's banner and click-through Internet models
6. A new product made possible by "servicizing"
7. A new role your firm could take through forward integrating into your customers' businesses
8. A way in which a supplier of yours might disintermediate you in a marketing or distribution channel
9. A way in which your business could reduce costs through backward integration in your supply chain
10. One way in which each of the following technologies could be used to enable new business strategy by your organization:
    a. High-speed computing
    b. Broadband, wireless, narrowcasting, and ubiquitous computing
    c. Data mining

The Digital Alchemy® Process:

INNOVATE

The Digital Alchemist® seeks opportunities to exploit information technology in ways not envisioned by competitors. In a time of disruptive change, such as we face today, our immediate challenge is not to succumb to simple, incremental improvement. We need to go beyond "faster, better, cheaper." We need to ask our-

How Does Your Business Strategy Address Channel Management and Your Channel Roles?

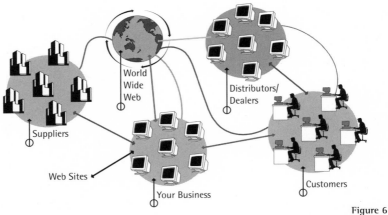

Figure 6

selves, "How can we take the new capabilities that technology is enabling, such as providing virtually unlimited network capacity at very low — nearly zero — cost, and change the very heart of how we do business?" Nearly every aspect of the way we live, work, play and think is about to change.

We also need to keep an eye on the competitive landscape as these changes are affecting the roles of the players in our marketing and distribution channels.

Some have said that the Internet is the great disintermediator. Clearly, that is not correct. The Internet has, in fact, spawned a new generation of intermediaries, such as Yahoo, Google, and many others. What the Internet *has* done is expose players who are not adding value.

It is critical that you analyze these channel dynamics and realign your business to continually add more value for your customers. This might be achieved through such means as vendor-managed inventory or solution marketing (e.g., supplying a seventy-two degree building rather than just supplying power).

Sample best practice companies include:
- 3M
- Intel
- Virgin Entertainment Group (U.K.)
- Bose Corporation
- Hewlett-Packard
- WorldWide Access
- Ernst & Young
- Medtronic
- Yahoo

Anticipating Change and Proactively Innovating Strategy

Over the years, I have developed a number of approaches to both the challenge of anticipating change and innovating strategy. Three of the most successful approaches for my clients have been: the phantom supercompetitor, the innovation pyramid, and scenario-based accelerated gameplanning environment (SAGE).

The Phantom Supercompetitor

This approach calls for a working group to brainstorm the attributes of a supercompetitor — a company that would be seen as their greatest nightmare. While subject to all of the normal business environment conditions as they are, the phantom would have none of its behavioral or cultural baggage. The supercompetitor would begin with all of the knowledge held by your company and would

New Supercompetitor Targets (Your Business)

*Your Greatest
Nightmare Is a Reality!*

Figure 7

leverage the best technology and processes to create a lean, mean, competitive machine.

To get things started, the working group should assume they just received today's newspaper announcing a supercompetitor is targeting their company. A working group should be broken into teams of seven to ten people and each should complete a template with this information: company weaknesses, opportunities to exploit those weaknesses, and the technology-enabled accelerators for achieving identified opportunities.

Table 4: Supercompetitor Template

Weaknesses at Old Company "The Soft Underbelly"	Opportunities to Exploit Weaknesses	Technology-enabled Accelerators for the Achievement of Identified Opportunities

For each weakness identified at the old company, the teams identify an opportunity for the phantom competitor to create an advantage and then develop a list of initiatives needed to achieve the opportunity. At the end, the teams are brought together to report back to the group. Then, a facilitator asks the entire group to change hats and consider the best strategic countermeasures their current employer could take to prevent the nightmare.

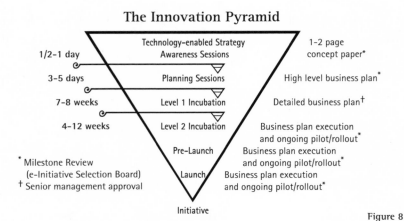

Figure 8

The Innovation Pyramid

This is an approach for organizations that want to encourage increased grassroots understanding of strategy. It is for organizations that accept this precept: While change must be encouraged and driven from the top, down; innovation is truly a bottoms-up process. Figure 8 illustrates the way the process operates.

All organization employees can be encouraged to attend an initial awareness session. From there on, they must complete the work on the right-hand side of the diagram and pass the specified review in order to move on. Reward and recognition systems must be applied to this approach to encourage the level of work and innovation required for success.

Scenario-based Accelerated Gameplanning Environment (SAGE)

As its name suggests, SAGE is a scenario-based environment. In the not-so-distant past, the rate of change was slow enough so that linear strategic planning was generally sufficient. Today, the rate of change has accelerated to such a point that too many of the variables on the competitive landscape are unpredictable. The question becomes one of managing during uncertain times with insufficient information. SAGE is an approach that proactively addresses this situation.

The organizational steps include selecting an executive sponsor who can ensure the project stays true to the goals and objectives of the business, selecting a governing group of three to five members of senior management who can serve as a kind of board of directors (e.g., receiving periodic reports, providing buy-in and approval from key corporate sectors), and selecting a cross-disciplinary working group.

In the next step, the working group identifies the key trends (e.g., economic, technological, socio-political, regulatory, etc.) that could impact the organization, as well as the drivers of their business (e.g., brand, price elasticity, etc.). Then they complete a competitor analysis. Outside consultants with expertise in each of the respective areas may assist during this step.

Scenarios are then created. A scenario is essentially a narrative that describes a future in which the organization might find itself doing business. Best practice calls for the development of three to five scenarios. Fewer than three leaves too many unaddressed possibilities and greater than five is usually too difficult for us to fully embrace. Each should be robust, however. No one scenario is going to actually be the future that your organization will face. If we knew that, we wouldn't need multiple scenarios. What we need to ensure is that all scenarios, when taken in their entirety, include all plausible (note the use of "plausible" and not "possible" or "likely") business conditions the organization may have to confront.

Once the scenarios are developed, the working group needs to agree on the metrics for success. In most companies, these metrics already exist (e.g., X% ROI, Y% ROA, number one or two in every market served, etc.). The working group can then be divided into teams (one per scenario) and sent off to develop the compelling vision, strategy, and specific, actionable initiatives required for the organization to achieve the success metrics in their particular scenario. In a truly drastic scenario, the best recommendation could be the sale of the business while its value is still high. Or, strategies could include alliances with third parties, or the introduction of new products, services, and processes. This is where the Digital Alchemists® really shine.

SAGE: Managing in Uncertain Times

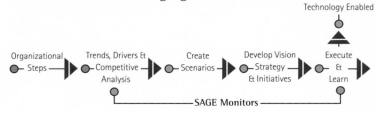

Figure 9

In the end, all of the strategies and initiatives are reviewed by a supervisory subset of the working group. The initiatives are classified and those that survive this review are assigned out to the working group to determine such matters as:

- What are the measurable benefits of this initiative?
- What are the costs and other resource requirements?
- Under what circumstances would this initiative be executed?
- Based upon the length of time it takes to prepare and practice the initiative, when should work begin on it?
- What risks are associated with the initiative?

After reviewing all of the initiatives, metrics are selected and tied to the preparation and execution of each.

All of this information is brought together and assembled into the SAGE gameplan. Using the gameplan, an executive can manage in real-time by monitoring the SAGE metrics and determining what action was predecided. No coach would go into a game without scouting the other team and knowing what to do under various game conditions. The SAGE process and gameplan give Digital Alchemist® executives that same competitive edge.

However, beware the single biggest obstacle to innovation — *phagonovoideasis.*

Most organizations have hundreds of good ideas. The problem is that these ideas usually threaten someone's turf. Whether seen as a threat to power, resources, or status, new concepts in an organization are like foreign bodies in the blood stream. The body's immune system responds and engulfs them in a process called phagocytosis (*phago* -engulf; *cytosis* -cell). Phagonovoideasis is simply the organization's immune response to the new idea (*phago* - engulf; *novo* -new; *ideasis* -idea) — that is, the organizational white cells kill the new idea and retain the status quo.

Leverage Anywhere, Anytime Wireless Communications

Today, when a child goes to daycare, mom and dad can watch them through tiny digital cameras connected to the Internet. And, in the United Kingdom, some stores have placed these miniature cameras in the eyes of people on cereal boxes to monitor shoplifting.

Appliance and other hardware manufacturers are already beginning to put IP (Internet protocol) addresses in their equipment as the smart house becomes a reality. An IP address makes that equipment available for contact over the Internet. If you are working late, you could contact your living room lights over the Internet and turn them on as easily as flipping the switch in person. Or, you could start the microwave and have dinner ready when you get home — even to adjust the settings if you get caught in unexpected traffic.

Broadband, Wireless, and Internet 2
Anytime Anyplace Anyhow Anyone Anything — Always On!

Internet 2, an advanced computer network already being used in experiments, offers a high-speed, fiber optic line backbone that can send data from 2.4 to as fast as 9.6 billion bits per second

Figure 10

All of these addressable devices, wireless telecommunications including the global positioning system (GPS), DirecTV, personal communication systems (PCS), radio frequency (RF), and cellular will offer substantial opportunities for new services.

We are rapidly approaching the point where technology and the cyberpsychographics of convenience will converge. Broadband will mean far more than just the ability to download movies in much the same way as people download music today. It will mean *always on*— broadcasting, narrowcasting, and receiving at very high speeds.

The way business is conducted and promoted will be profoundly changed by these developments in telecommunications. There is already more data traffic in our networks than voice. Soon, there will be more machine to machine communications than human to human. What new services can your organization create leveraging these capabilities? Organizations with mobile assets (e.g., trucks, train cars, and containers) can know where they are at all times. Suppliers can enhance their relationships with buyers by creating smart, wireless reordering systems. Dematerializing the wire and the product by adding knowledge creates a powerful combination.

Profit from Invisibly Embedded Intelligence

Flash back to 1902. You are flipping through the pages of the popular Sears catalog, when you come across several advertisements for motors. You need one of these clunky machines, the ads declare, to speed up the many tasks and chores you perform around the house and farm. All kinds of attachments are available to adapt the motor for specific jobs.

Return to the present and motors, of course, are ubiquitous. Today, most homes have fifty different motors. But you won't see ads promoting them. Instead, we see ads for refrigerators, washers, dryers, dishwashers, and vacuum cleaners, with no mention of the motors inside. We take it for granted that everything that requires a mechanical engine indeed comes equipped with one.

Embedded Computing
Chips in Everything—Communication with Each Other

Electronic Paper that can turn a hand-
written note into transmittable e-mail

Credit cards that announce your presence
to a department store

Cookware that never allows its contents
to burn

Figure 11

But look at today's ads for personal computers. Reminiscent of the motors of yesteryear, they are pictured as clunky information engines that are sold by companies that promote the many applications they can perform and the attachments that help them work. "In the future," says MIT Media Lab director Nicholas Negroponte, "the PC will be blown to bits." Just like the motor, the microchip will spread everywhere.

In the automotive world we are already seeing microchips containing microelectromechanical sensors (MEMS). They are embedded into tires to warn us when their air pressure is getting low, in engines to anticipate problems while they can still be easily corrected, and they are used to deploy airbags. Chips are already in many hotel doorknobs and will eventually make their way into everyday objects such as pots, pans, and chairs. Indeed, the spaghetti sauce might never burn again because the pot will be smart enough to know when to turn the stove off. Our refrigerators might even call us at work to let us know that we are running low on milk and should stop at the market on the way home.

We may even see batteries in our shoe heels that would generate a charge as we walk to power our own Personal Area Networks.

Microchips might even be sewn into our clothing, assisting the blind, color-blind, or style-challenged by enabling our clothes to know what goes together with what, even when we do not.

Consider how your organization could radically change its current products by embedding intelligence into them.

Leverage Information about Information

Many organizations have digital assets lying around that they either underutilize or walk right past every day. It is critical for a successful information age organization to inventory its digital assets and determine how they can be creatively used.

Once you have a handle on the information assets your organization holds, you can begin to exploit those assets in innovative ways. Many companies already do this in their respective industries. One of the best known is *TV Guide*, which publishes information (schedules, etc.) about information (television programming). Remarkably, *TV Guide* has been known to make higher profits than the three major TV networks combined. But there are many new examples in the digital age. Directory services on the World Wide Web, such as Yahoo and InfoSeek, that enable users of the Internet to search and find Web sites of interest (again, information about information) are enjoying a great deal of success, primarily from advertisers who want to reach people when they embark on a search. For example, in some years American Airlines makes more money from its Sabre online flight information and reservation system than they do from actually flying passengers. Less obvious examples can be found in almost any organization. An energy company, for instance, could make its gas and electric usage data available as a product to appliance companies and equipment manufacturers interested in better understanding their customers and in using the feedback to build more efficient machines.

The Bose Corporation recognized that it had information about the way its stereo speakers perform in all kinds of buildings and conditions. It turned that information into knowledge by creating a software package that simulates what a speaker setup will sound like just from the blueprints of the room. Now, potential customers can enter the specifications of their listening space into the program and receive an audio and graphical simulation of how certain speakers would sound. The software uses color intensity to represent the way the sound travels. Bose can sell this software or just use it for a sales and marketing edge.

Trane, the global heating and air conditioning (HVAC) company, recognized that the closer the decision to purchase HVAC equipment was to the date the equipment had to be installed, the more the decision would be based solely on price. As a result, it took its extensive knowledge of the way HVAC equipment operates in a multitude of environments and conditions and created selection software and CAD templates that would dovetail right into its customers' systems. The point behind leveraging such information is to get closer to the customers, cause them to think about Trane much earlier in the process, and turn an otherwise commodity, price-based transaction into a relationship sale.

16
011000

Create Personalized Customer Experiences

Your customers are using the Internet (or would if given a good reason) and you would like to somehow leverage that use into enhancing your relationships and getting closer to them. One intriguing approach is to create a dematerialized, virtual presence in their office by providing them with a computer desktop platform, specifically designed for what they do and becoming an industry-specific, knowledge-based, value-added broadcaster.

USA Today NewsTracker (www.infogate.com), the successor to PointCast, a California-based company, developed an information platform that becomes a customer's computer desktop and screensaver while simultaneously responding to a customer-generated profile by providing real-time stock quotes, trade information, news, weather, sports, and other information of interest to that specific

The Advent of Personalization

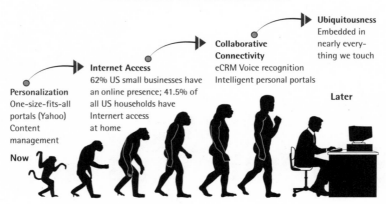

Ubiquitousness
Embedded in
nearly every-
thing we touch

Collaborative
Connectivity
eCRM Voice recognition
Intelligent personal portals

Internet Access
62% US small businesses have
an online presence; 41.5% of
all US households have
Internert access
at home

Personalization
One-size-fits-all
portals (Yahoo)
Content
management

Now

Later

Figure 12

customer. There is no charge to the customer for the service. Info-gate makes its money from advertisers.

We are beginning to see businesses take the Infogate concept to the next level by creating customized computer desktops for their customers and using those desktops to channel specific information regarding their products and services to the customer. A gas and electric utility might provide such a desktop for facility manager customers with various calculators, software, and other products and services geared to that customer. By intrusive profiling (i.e., asking questions of the customer) or nonintrusive profiling (i.e., monitoring usage from the server and developing a profile on its own), the company can gain much more information about its customers to target content, offerings, products, and services specifically to them. It's a win for the company because they are getting their message directly out to their customer on a targeted, real-time, and low-cost basis. It's a win for the customer because they are getting information specifically aimed at them and at improving their performance.

17
010001

There ain't no Such Thing as a Web Page

Most of us have an interesting habit of transposing old technologies onto new ones. For instance, when we think about the capability of a car's engine we use the term horsepower. Yet, yoking up 350 horses to a Toyota is truly unimaginable. The term Web page is quite similar – it carries with it the constraints of the old technology and that can hold us back.

A page is a document produced by a press, copier, or the like. Its size is limited by the size of its source. Its scope is limited to two dimensions – height and width. When we refer to Web pages we frequently limit our thinking to those same constraints. For that reason we see that most web sites today are little more than brochure-ware – two dimensional sites that could have easily been produced using the old technology. In fact, they are even worse than printed pages since their print equivalent requires no batteries or power cord, can be of substantially higher resolution, and can be folded and taken anywhere.

Many Web pages do not take advantage of the many capabilities the Internet has to offer — such as interactivity, connectivity to related documents, and personalization. In fact, Web pages do not exist. The Internet enables us to serve content to a screen. Based on input from the viewer or information known about the viewer, that content can be personalized to such an extent that no two viewers share exactly the same customer experience. Thinking differently about the semantics can also lead us to think in new ways about adding value to the customer experience.

Don't be constrained by yesterday's thinking

The Internet Is Changing Advertising from Active to Passive

Interactive media, including the Web, offer opportunities to dramatically change the current business model and challenge the most basic assumptions governing what we now think of as advertising. Today's banner ads may become pay-for-results ads in which a set fee is paid for each qualified customer that the advertising platform (portal, online magazine, etc.) sends to the advertiser's Web site. This could be augmented by the amount of time the consumer stays on the advertiser's site. The advertising platform could simply take a percentage of sales generated by its referral. In this sense, advertisements in cyberspace would be like salesmen and the owners of the ad space might keep the commission.

Today, the most prominent models for Internet advertising are the banner ad and click-throughs. Banner ads are essentially billboards for advertisers that are placed on Web sites likely to be trafficked by their customers (e.g., Yahoo and other directories and ESPNET and other content sites). They may include animation and usually are rectangular running from one side of the screen to the other. They are generally priced on a traditional print and broadcast model such as cost per million. Click-throughs are a special instance of a banner ad in which pricing is based on the number of users who click on the banner through to the advertiser's site. Click-through charges generally range from $0.30 to $1.40 each. Variations on these themes include clickable buttons and ads tied to certain content (e.g., a certain Yahoo keyword search generates a certain ad).

It is important to note that when distribution channels change, substantial business opportunities are frequently created for organizations that move quickly (e.g., overnight package delivery and Federal Express, television mail order and QVC, and catalog sales and Sears).

Marketers are not on the Web for exposure, but for results. Picture the process of prospecting for customers as a giant funnel. Traditional mass-market advertising on TV and radio as well as in national newspapers and magazines work at or near the wide mouth of the funnel. No ad on a Web site will ever provide the mass exposure of those media. But where the Web works its wonders is at the bottom, or spout, of the funnel. The Web can actually deliver a fully qualified lead or customer.

Rich Everett, then manager of interactive communications for Chrysler Corporation told *Wired* (4.02) that there are four steps to landing a customer: tell, sell, link, and think. A traditional ad, he says, will tell you that a product exists and sell you on its benefits. The Web, however, must pick up where traditional ads leave off. If Chrysler does its job on the Web, he says, it will link qualified and interested buyers into a virtual showroom and give them enough information to think whether they are actually going to purchase the car.

In this model, a new way of placing and buying ads must be put in place. Advertisers such as Chrysler should not necessarily pay up front for the space on the digital pages of, say, *Time* magazine. Perhaps they should pay only for the results — for instance, a set fee for each qualified customer that *Time* sends to Chrysler's Web site.

Add a New Dimension to Your Sales and Marketing Initiatives

California homebuilder Presley Homes sold new houses without building a single model home. In 1997, Presley used an eight thousand dollar, computer-generated home simulation program to virtually walk a client through what their home would look like. The initial experiment with the program resulted in Presley Homes completely selling out a thirty-eight-unit subdivision in three months. Many consumers find it difficult to envision what a house, furniture, automobile, or other product might look like in a different color, style, or other version from the one "on the floor," and sellers find it too expensive or in some cases physically impossible to stock all of the variations. Using 3-D modeling and simulation software, sellers can create highly realistic virtual products. While more and more consumers will be willing to buy in this way – elim-

Figure 13

inating the need for on-hand inventory, model homes, and demo cars — even those who are not will be able to reduce the buying cycle by eliminating products and styles they do not like. Rather than be shown forty houses, many of which may not meet your desires, you could take computer-based virtual house tours and only visit the few that are really of interest.

Panoramic digital cameras and other technology are already being introduced that enable buyers to stay at home and experience the merchandise — from taking a test drive to checking out hotels and cruise ships for vacation ideas. Organizations that take a leading role in this area will be able to capture the imagination of their buyers. For situations when downloading images from the Internet is too slow, CDs can be created for around one dollar a piece that hold up to 650 megabytes of movies and graphics that can be integrated with the Internet to offer full interactivity.

Learn to Write for Machines

Finding the information you are looking for can be quite a challenge in cyberspace. Searching the Internet and most databases requires that you precisely match the query and the result — character for character (e.g., Boolean search engines). The Internet and online services are searchable by keyword, but a keyword search only works when you know exactly what you are looking for. For example, a search for "Toyota" will return documents containing the word "Toyota". However, a search for "imported car" will only return documents with "Toyota" in them if they also contain the phrase "imported car". The responsibility for being found still rests upon the content creator. A thesaurus can improve accuracy (e.g., if the thesaurus equates "man", "human," and "person," then a query using the word "man" will return results as if all three terms had been used

Table 5: XML

- **A better way to tag content.**
  Today a keyword search can return thousands of possibilities. Tomorrow XML tags will filter data and return only the results you want.
- **A better way to distribute and track information.**
  Today it is difficult to republish content across many sites, and more difficult to track who is reading it. Tomorrow XML will make both a snap.
- **A better way to do business.**
  Today you can browse catalogs on-line. Tomorrow XML tags will allow data to be customized just for you.
- **A better way to do business... on the road.**
  Today Web graphics bog down and slow Internet connections. Tomorrow your notebook will download only material tagged as text.

```
<?XML version= "1.0"?>
<xmldoc>
<customer>
<accountid>
AE4-Robertson </accountid>
  <name>
  <first> Eric </first>
  <mi> H </mi>
<last> Robertson </last>
  </name>
  <title> VP Sales </title>
  <contact>
  <wphone> 123-555-1212 </wphone>
  <hphone> 1130-555-5678 </hphone>
  <email> salesvp@yoyo.com </email>
  </contact>
  </customer>
  </xmldoc>
```

in the query) but does not solve the problem entirely and can be difficult to create and maintain.

This means that to get the most out of today's search engines we need to compose content not just for the human reader but also for the machine reader that will navigate through cyberspace and bring back possible hits. If the machine does not make a connection, the human will never even have the chance to do so.

The way to write for machines is to classify and label, or tag, your content (e.g., add human-invisible but machine-readable tags to the "Toyota" content that include the words "car," "import," "Japanese company," etc.). A key enabler of content tagging is eXtensible Markup Language (XML).

XML offers much more than just tagging. XML enables legacy computer databases to be connected to web sites so that changes in the database could be reflected on the Web site automatically and in real time. For example, pricing data can be modeled, entered into a legacy database, and then automatically populated in Web sites.

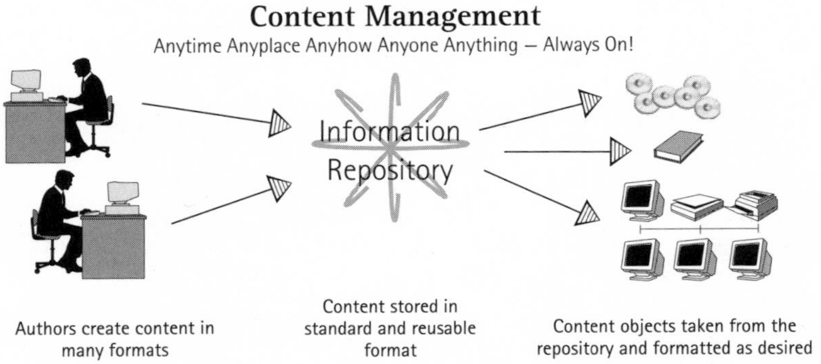

Content Management
Anytime Anyplace Anyhow Anyone Anything — Always On!

| Authors create content in many formats | Content stored in standard and reusable format | Content objects taken from the repository and formatted as desired |

Information Repository

Figure 14

XML can also be used to make the way content is stored or represented in a database independent from the way it is used. This makes it easier to repurpose content. Most word processing software stores its content in a proprietary format requiring conversion for use by other programs. Content that is stored in a format independent from use does not have this problem. Because XML makes independent content representation possible it can also enable enhanced workflow management and multiple media output.

The next generation of search and retrieval engines will go beyond the capabilities and limitations of today's Boolean and thesaurus-based tools, removing some of this burden from the content creator. Several promising approaches are on the horizon. One considers the query term (e.g., "man") as a point in space. Around that point and radiating outward are all of the words that are close to the same meaning as "man." We would expect to see "human," "person," "woman," "child," and so forth in close proximity to "man." Thus, a context-based search would specify a certain radius from the point of the query term and use all of those words in conducting its search. In that way, the searcher does not need to know exactly what they are looking for. Other techniques include statistical searching and other grammatical algorithms.

Explore opportunities to create customized market-of-one customer experiences.

Put Software Agents to Work

Software agents are computer programs that can be used to perform specific tasks on behalf of their users. One consumer and business use of agents is to find the lowest price for a given product or service. Another is to pull information by conducting searches through multiple databases. Another interesting use for agents is as an online gatekeeper.

Going back only a few years ago, florists, real estate professionals, banks, and many others would have been hard pressed to consider American Airlines a competitor. Yet today, if I buy, sell, or finance a house through an approved American Airline provider I will receive frequent flier miles based on the value of the house. That can be a valuable differentiator, a powerful market targeting device (American's Frequent Flyers), and an effec-

Table 6: Agents

Today:	
• Providing information	
• Product and service marketing	
• Company prices	**Stages of Buying Behavior**
• Accepting orders	• Need identification ⎫ Agent-
	• Product brokering ⎬ mediated
Tomorrow:	• Merchant brokering ⎭ today
• Machine-to-machine electronic markets	• Negotiation
	• Purchase & delivery
• Empowererd agents that transact business from sourcing through negotiation through tracking receipt of goods	• Service & evaluation

tive use of one of American's digital assets – its frequent flyer system and the relationships it has developed. American has become a gatekeeper for many products and services that they do not own or control. Yet, they profit when they source business to one of their partners.

While frequent flyer miles are a potent lever, there are other motivators to consider. Both in business-to-business and consumer transactions, buyers have said they are looking for timeliness, accuracy, quality, and convenience. You could create a simple software agent for your customers to use in purchasing products that could also link to third party products – a gatekeeper application – offering one-stop shopping and establishing you as a channel captain. A moving and storage company could create the *Relocating Your Home* and the *Relocating Your Business* agents. A bank could create the *Managing Your Treasury* agent and an insurance company could create the *Managing Your Risks* agent. Each agent is a one-stop shop covering all aspects of the area from the customer's perspective.

You should also consider software agents from a defensive perspective. If you compete on a basis other than price, you may want to consider blocking others' agents so that you have the opportunity to tell a bigger story than a simple price comparison.

Extend Your Brand into Cyberspace

In the January 2000 issue of *Red Herring*, venture capitalist Bill Davidow differentiated branding from achieving mindshare through marketing by saying, "For a terrible analogy, the Unabomber got tremendous mindshare, but I don't think he was a brand."

Everyone understands the value of establishing a brand name in any marketplace. Well-known brands almost always command a premium price. The Levi's image creates more demand for its jeans. The *Time* magazine image creates more currency for its news reports. In cyberspace, you might assume that these brands would fade away. After all, the Internet creates a level playing field for new businesses to establish themselves.

But the reality is to the contrary. In the physical world, it can cost a great deal of money to have the right address or a lavish storefront;

Be Brand Intensive, Not Capital Intensive

Brand is one facet to differentiate as products and serviced commodities

AT&T has proven the value of a national brand with its One Rate® program

Branding is becoming sustainable identity

Net brands can be created — many market facings mean it can be both global and local

"It's imperative for companies to focus on new products, managing brands and building market share." — John Byran, CEO, Sara Lee

Figure 15

on the Internet you and your competitors, both old and new, have the opportunity to look the same. As a result, your brand name, trademark, logos, and overall image take on heightened importance in this world where everything seems up for grabs. A company's history and reputation will become more and more important for success in cyberspace, serving as indicators of quality and reliability and saving your customer time and risk — they know what to expect.

Lexus has extended their brand into cyberspace by providing a concierge to greet its Web site visitors at the Lexus Centre of Performing Arts and then guide them through the site. The Web site created by the Saturn car company encourages owners to register their names and personal information, look up the names of other Saturn owners in their town, and communicate with them. "The Saturn sales proposition is based on this community of owners," says Tom Wang, marketing manager for Saturn's online ad agency, Organic Online Inc. "The subliminal message is that you are a better person because you are a member of this club. Everyone wants to belong to something." This approach enables Saturn to extend its image of being "A Different Kind of Company." Another example is the Web site created by Ragu. A visit to this site evokes all things Italian. You can visit Mama Cucina's kitchen and swap recipes. And visitors don't necessarily talk about pasta sauces all the time; they discuss Italian cooking and culture in general. Such an experience often fosters a deep bond with the products and brand name.

23

Productizing and Servicizing: Ernie and the Pacemakers

The rapidly decreasing costs of telecommunications along with the widespread and growing adoption of the Internet is enabling the merger of products and services. A pacemaker, for instance, could be equipped with a wireless transmitter that sends your respiratory data and heart beat patterns to a 24/7, world-class cardiac monitoring service. Imagine the appeal of such a service to someone who has just had a heart attack. The subscription to that service would be a key differentiator for the product. When the lines between product and service blur, the results may well be higher profit margins than when a business remains solely a product company. Knowledge can be "productized" by being packaged into a software program or made available through an online information service.

Ernst & Young (E&Y), the well-known accounting, auditing, and consulting firm, recognized that many small- to medium-sized businesses did not consider doing business with E&Y because they assumed it would be too costly. Yet these firms represented a market that E&Y wanted to attract — both for today's business as well as to position itself for the future when these organizations had grown into large firms. They decided to make more than one hundred previously internal databases available to subscribers for an annual fee of $6,000. Additionally, if a subscriber could not find the answer they sought, they could submit a question to this service, known as "Ernie," and they would receive a reply within forty-eight business hours. E&Y sold about seven thousand subscriptions in the first year. With virtually no additional expense E&Y, a professional services business, was making nearly $42 million from the licensing of an intellectual, capital-based, knowledge product.

Dematerialization is resulting in this blurring of products and services and creating digital opportunities to be exploited.

24
011000

Collaborative Systems: Be Here, Be There and Be Effective

In addition to products, services, and process, even people are dematerializing. When a company finds that it employs more and more telecommuters, the technological infrastructure must compensate for the infrequency of face-to-face contact. Voice mail and e-mail only go so far. That's why all companies should develop collaborative virtual workspaces that:

- Facilitate real-time sharing
- Enable joint authoring, commenting, and annotation
- Enable joint negotiation and development of the form and content of the information
- Provide a common context for the work
- Exploit corporate data and knowledge

Such workspaces are essentially networking minds together in ways never before possible. The first step in building such a workspace is to think about your information-sharing architecture. David Reed, former chief technology officer for Lotus Development Corporation, says that such an architecture should be composed of what he calls the "5 Ps:" First, you need to settle on tools for exchanging complex digital documents, or *paper*. Then, you need to concentrate on *plumbing* issues, such as your network setup, resource administration, and security. The way online information is organized into user *portfolios* is the third key issue. Should the information be sorted according to work teams, or by customer? The *people* in the virtual workspace must be able to take on different roles — as experts on a certain subject, or as anonymous but constructive complainers at other times. Finally, the *processes* that the company performs must be set up online in a way that encourages collaboration.

Applications for this practice include providing training, developing proposals with a global cast of experts from within your organization as well as outside of it, conducting a marketing presentation for a customer, or idea brainstorming with resources from around the world in real time. There are countless other examples, the key is to look for opportunities where the best minds are simply not co-located simultaneously.

While collaborative systems rarely make a substantial reduction in travel expenses, they do lower the threshold for communicating and sharing knowledge, resulting in better products and services. In the *Harvard Business Review*, Rosabeth Moss Kanter wrote (of these practices): "I call it a company's collaborative advantage... A well-developed ability to create and sustain fruitful collaborations gives [organizations] a significant competitive leg up."

Let's look at an example from Harley Davidson of Milwaukee. They developed an interactive quality assurance collaborative system using video and document-sharing technology between three sites to link their design, manufacturing, and QA engineering teams. The new technology enables these teams to replace sequential paper review processes with real-time collaboration. With the new process, design, manufacturing, and QA engineers work out their product goals and methods during video and document-sharing sessions three to eight times a week. As a result, the company has significantly reduced product development time while improving product quality.

On the horizon we can expect to see:

- "Share-aware" software applications that allow multiple people in multiple locations to work on the same document simultaneously.
- Tools that provide collaborators with more intelligent assistance. For example, discovering relevant collaborators and information for specific tasks and explaining the context of a collaboration quickly so new team members can get up to speed.
- Software agents that initiate and facilitate collaboration, from screening and forwarding relevant information to routing forms as part of a business process.
- Tools that exploit visualization technology to enhance the effectiveness of collaborations, including video archive and retrieval, video e-mail, and multimedia annotation techniques.
- Archiving tools that allow participants to review the contents of a meeting after it has happened or before joining it midstream.

MASTERING DIGITAL ALCHEMY®

As a Digital Alchemist®, you should now be able to envision:

1. An agenda for a workshop to brainstorm new strategies
2. Wireless communications creating new ways of working with your customers and your field salesforce
3. How ubiquitous intelligence can create new product or service opportunities for your business
4. How to use information about information to create new revenue

5. How to create personalized customer experiences
6. How to personalize your customers' Internet experience
7. How to turn the Web into a bidirectional focus group
8. How to recognize phagonovoideasis and how to combat it
9. How to go beyond 2-D brochureware to create 3-D Webware
10. How eXtensible Markup Language (XML) can benefit your business

The Digital Alchemy® Process:

ALIGN

The industrial age focused on a centralized, hierar-
chically structured, command and control organization.
Such an organization was well suited to assembly line
mass-production. Information age businesses are moving away from this structure. They are recognizing that
rather than owning all aspects of a business, they can

focus on just the parts they do best (e.g., Nike made no shoes last year — instead, they focused on product and brand management) and develop strategic relationships with others to do the rest. The telecommunications revolution significantly empowered this trend by enabling the "wiring-up" of all of the businesses in this networked organization. This chapter focuses on these issues and offers nine digital practices for today's organizations to consider.

Sample best practice companies include:

- Adaptec, Inc.
- Federal Express
- National Semiconductor
- Boston Beer Company
- Isadra, Inc.
- Nike
- Cisco
- GE Power
- Oracle

25
011001

Different Carrots Drive New Behaviors

New information technologies are changing the way we get work done. From technology-enhanced customer relationships to telecommuting we are asking workers to stop doing things the old way and adopt new processes. But if we motivate, reward, and recognize them based on the old ways of doing things, it shouldn't be surprising that these technologies fail because we do not see the desired changes in the people who must make them work. We must determine the behaviors and culture our organizations need and then determine how to foster them.

For decades (if not longer) we have compensated people based on the scarcity of their knowledge. The more rare the knowledge, the higher the compensation — thus fast food clerks are paid far less than surgeons. However, as we implement collaborative systems in the workplace, it becomes critical for us to encourage knowledge sharing. Based on the foundation of our compensation systems, employees will logically conclude that sharing knowledge threatens their employment while hoarding knowledge makes them more valuable. We need to change this culture and these behaviors to succeed in the information age.

Employees should be rewarded for sharing insights and information with other employees. When the company's unstated incentive system encourages information hoarding, employees think, "why should I let someone else take credit for my work?" But if employees are offered rewards, even as simple as a free dinner, they get the message that information sharing benefits everyone.

There is even value in the exchange of information regardless of the content exchanged, if for no other reason than because it begins to change behavior. So, as a starter, just encourage information sharing. Measure the number of discussion forum items created by individual employees and then measure the number of responses they create. (This provides at least some indication of the interest generated in the original item.) Then do the same for the responses. Continue to build on this until you are measuring the volume of all knowledge being exchanged electronically and the various branches of responses underneath. Recognize and reward those who are generating the most interest with their exchanges — even if the content does not seem valuable to you. Practice will change and, before long, valuable knowledge will be exchanged and new synergies will be established across the organization.

A government relations manager in a major European drug company was developing an information system to speed the process of regulatory filings. Little did he know that another employee down the hall had already created such a system. Separately, a researcher at the company was developing a presentation, complete with a series of twenty-five slides, to present to a scientific conference. He was unaware that a scientist in another department recently created a similar presentation when speaking at an outside lab. Employees, especially at big companies, are often reinventing the wheel — a costly and time-consuming problem.

The solution to this problem is not the same as the technical solution that enables knowledge sharing. The fundamental problem lies with culture and behavior — the people and how we manage them.

Determine the culture and behaviors needed to achieve your envisioned outcomes.

Agility: The Most Critical Skill of the Information Age

The way in which employment is structured and the skills necessary for success are just two of the profound changes occurring in the workplace. We are moving to a more flexible style of production quite unlike the highly routine mass-production of the industrial age. Management has begun to flatten. Middle management is being eliminated in many industries and in government services. Self-directed work teams are becoming more prevalent in industry and in government. Employees who once had compartmentalized, manual jobs on a production line with little or no contact with, dependence upon, or influence over other workers must now perform more wide-ranging tasks. They rely more on automation and communication and use technologies that allow fast and precise communication.

Organizations can now consist of large but fluctuating and diffuse networks of suppliers, manufacturers, marketers, designers, and so forth. Technology and communication now allow businesses to control production elements at a distance, thus distributing and avoiding risk.

The large corporation may remain, but work will be distributed among the various interdependent partners, and that distribution will change periodically as production needs change. This environment makes individual jobs less secure and requires skills to be more portable.

Market preferences have also changed. Customers, both international and local, now want and can obtain much more than price. As Anthony Carnevale said in *America in the New Economy: How New Competitive Standards Are Radically Changing America's Workplaces*: "In the old economy competitive success was based almost exclusively on the ability to improve productivity. In the new economy organization and nations compete not only on their ability to improve productivity but on their ability to deliver quality, variety, customization, convenience, and timeliness as well."

With the accelerated changes the digital transformation is bringing, what should organizations be looking for when hiring employees? Let's consider some of the key skill sets employers should be seeking out.

Agility

Employees are increasingly required to learn how to use new equipment, new software, new products, or new procedures. Because different employees learn differently, employees and their managers must learn how each employee learns best, through doing or reading, individually or in a group, at work or away. Reading a manual will be pointless for some, while others will devour it.

Bill Gates has said that he hires people at Microsoft more for their potential than for their experience. In other words, he wants people who show an ability to learn and adapt to new situations quickly. Since the software industry changes so fast, relying too heavily on what is listed on resumes can be dangerous. Sometimes experience can get in the way of approaching new problems and integrating new knowledge.

This is becoming increasingly true for all industries. The business world is changing so fast that people who can capitalize on new opportunities will tend to do better than those who have simply mastered an old process. Career paths, in general, should be mirroring changes in the business world at large. An advertising executive who can pick up the new principles of how advertising works on the World Wide Web, for instance, will be much better off than someone who only knows the old advertising models.

Communication Skills
In order to work in teams, to customize for clients, and to respond appropriately to inquires from within or without the organization, employees must be able to communicate clearly. This requires literacy and, increasingly, computational skills. Employees need to write clearly, not only getting the language right, but identifying what is important and expressing it with brevity and precision. With automation, much work shifts from *doing* to *watching* and *controlling* what machines do. This often requires an understanding of the formulas, charts, or tables used by the equipment and the ability to interpret and communicate that information.

Problem Solving
Working in an automated environment often involves monitoring and then solving problems as needed. Skills may be called upon most acutely when something goes wrong. Operators must not only understand the basic concepts and equipment involved, but must also know how to analyze unexpected problems, consult manuals, accurately describe problems to technical experts, and so on. This is as true for a plastics injection mold operator as for a public employee administering a database for a flood relief program. Such situations call for innovation and resourcefulness.

Listening Skills

Those whose work depends upon collaboration, or who are involved directly with customers, suppliers, or others must have the skill to listen. If competitiveness depends upon accurately meeting client needs, employees must learn how to listen for those needs. Similarly, collaborative work arrangements require good listening abilities because successful collaboration requires the clear transmission of messages between collaborators. Listening sounds like the easiest skill of all, but it is often lacking because many employees have been trained to tell, not to listen. This is particularly true for managers and supervisors.

Group Skills

Working in a group environment requires a series of "soft-skills" that go beyond listening. Collegiality is itself a learned skill. Individuals must learn to be assertive where necessary, but at the same time they must appreciate that aggressive and domineering behavior can hurt the team's effectiveness. Personal qualities like dependability, veracity, and conviviality also affect team performance. These are not so much skills to learn as qualities that one can learn to cultivate in the group. Understanding such group dynamics is itself an important skill. This is not only important within an enterprise. Increasingly, workers for one employer will spend their time problem solving with workers from client, customer, or supplier employers. Their ability to work collegially is part of the product.

Dispute Resolution Skills

Work remains a place of conflict. Employees get into conflicts with each other. Relations between the organization and its customers and suppliers can often involve conflict and it's necessary to resolve that conflict if productive relations are to continue. Conflicts will still arise between those who manage and those whose work is the subject of that management. The way this conflict is dealt with can have a profound effect on morale and success. Employees (whether managerial or not) increasingly need to understand the dynamics of conflict and the cost of unresolved conflict. They need techniques for getting to the bottom of problems and solving them.

Cultural Sensitivity
The U.S. is increasingly trading in the world market, whether it is judicial systems in the new Ukraine, cattle breeding in Argentina, or oil and gas technology in Indonesia. Ours is also a multicultural community. Employees need to develop the ability to work with people from diverse backgrounds, not just in the passive sense of tolerating diversity, but in the active sense of collaborating together to get work done. Increasingly, overseas customers will measure our competitiveness by how we are able to work effectively in their culture. Few countries have such a good training ground at home.

Computer Literacy
Most employees in the next decade will need computer literacy. This will present less challenge to the Nintendo generation. However, for workers unskilled in the rescue of electronic princesses, lack of familiarity with the computer as a tool can present a major barrier to retraining. One of the more discouraging aspects of computer literacy is the lack of recognition for generic skills. Many computer applications are quite similar yet we still tend to measure skills in terms of experience on specific applications. This denies employees credit for their experience and makes their skills seem less portable than they are.

In an age when computer programs are upgraded to new versions almost annually, what is important is not experience on Microsoft Office 2000, but the degree of versatility and understanding that the individual has in using the computer to deal with real workplace issues. We should develop new ways of measuring competency in this important area. This would help to facilitate retraining for those without such skills and to facilitate improved portability of and recognition of these skills once acquired.

Career Development Skills

If work is indeed becoming more transient, then a necessary skill for survival in the workplace is to understand how one's career may develop and what can and should be done to keep abreast of change. An employee with career development skills is one who independently educates themselves for a rapidly changing tomorrow — not one who simply does what is necessary for today or even for their current employer. This is an issue of importance to the enterprise as well as to the individual employee. If change is an unavoidable reality, employees will fair best, and resist less, if they have realistic expectations about the changes they face, adequate warning, and meaningful opportunities to embrace lifelong learning. It is unrealistic to expect employers to be the sole source of training in this area. Employers train for the needs of their enterprise, not for the employee. Indeed, it is often the employer's lack of foresight, planning, expertise, or frankness that leaves employees without a job and any real means to retrain.

An enduring need of employees is not only to acquire skills, but to have the means to update those skills and to have them recognized. Increasingly, workers are learning on the job, through in-service training, by distance learning techniques, and other means. They are also taking courses to upgrade their skills. What we are lacking is a universally accepted means of assessing a person's training attainments through all these sources that will give employees recognition in the job market for their acquired competencies.

Knowledge Management Accelerates the Learning Curve

Much has been written about the shortage of computer programmers and other knowledge workers in the United States, but perhaps there is no such shortage. In fact, there may well be a surplus of unemployed knowledge workers.

The problem is that as the speed of technology changes and adoption has radically increased, there has been an inversely proportional decrease in the business life of the knowledge worker. An Assembly language programmer in the late 1960s could expect to be able to use those skills for another twenty or more years. Today's programmer has a career span that is much closer to that of the professional athlete. How long will today's Java language programmer be in high demand? Even five years sounds like a stretch. The solution lies in hiring an agile workforce and in training and retraining.

Knowledge workers are the keys to business success and should have minimum continuing education requirements to ensure they are remaining current on the latest developments in their fields.

Federal Express takes this issue seriously. They have deployed a human resources system that, among other features, offers its employees more than four thousand interactive courses. Employees can review job postings, decide how they want their careers to move forward, and then take the appropriate classes to achieve the desired growth. Upon completion of the training their records are updated.

Imagine taking this approach to another level by making employees responsible for ensuring that their resumes, including training, seminar attendance, and on-the-job and off-the-job experience (e.g., applicable volunteer work) are always up-to-date. At review time, the resume from the beginning of year could be compared to the resume from the end of year to determine the increase in skill level, contribution to the business, and so forth. Salary increases could be based on that value differentiation. What's more, it is always under the control of the employee.

Create New Roles in Your Organization

In 1959, in his book *Landmarks of Tomorrow*, Peter Drucker coined the term *knowledge worker* and predicted America's flip-flop of manufacturing work into primarily knowledge work. In 1994, in an *Atlantic Monthly* article titled, "The Age of Social Transformation," Drucker updated his own predictions and said: "By the end of this century, knowledge workers will make up a third or more of the workforce in the United States."

Drucker drove home rigorous criteria for true knowledge workers. He said they require "a good deal of formal education and the ability to acquire and to apply theoretical and analytical knowledge. Above all, they require the habit of continuous learning. Knowledge workers will not be the majority in the knowledge society, but...they will give the emerging knowledge society its character, its leadership, its social profile."

Even among the thought-leaders consulting in this area, we are treating knowledge management as if more than 60 percent of the workforce can find, understand, and interpret information on par with symbolic analysts. They can't. There is a knowledge work crisis brewing. A major gap is growing between what we're expecting and what the workforce can deliver. And, since knowledge is rapidly becoming the key determinant for business success, organizations will need to create special roles to fill this gap and promote the effective use and management of knowledge and intellectual capital. Some new roles will be developed to meet these needs.

- Knowledge acquirer — a person with either a psychology or sociology background who works with subject matter experts (from nuclear scientists to mailroom workers) to extract their job-related knowledge, including their all-important intuitive knowledge
- Knowledge representer — a systems architect who can take acquired knowledge and represent it in data structures that provide for ready access, ease-of-use, and efficient throughput
- Cybrarian — a guide to available digital resources who knows what is available, how to access it, and can assist in constructing the best queries; an expert in the field of knowledge navigation

Sixty to eighty percent of the American workforce cannot use data, information or knowledge as it is currently organized. In his 1991 book, *The Work of Nations: Preparing Ourselves for 21st Century Capitalism,* former U.S. Secretary of Labor Robert Reich said, "Essentially, three broad categories of work are emerging...routine production services, in-person services, and symbolic-analytic services." In his recoding of Adam Smith's *Wealth of Nations,* Reich describes symbolic analysts as the members of the workforce who "solve, identify, and broker problems by manipulating symbols. They simplify reality into abstract images that can be rearranged, juggled, experimented with, communicated to other specialists, and then, eventually, transformed back into reality." He listed these problem-solvers and information brokers as everyone from software developers to investment bankers to film-makers. Reich also said, "Symbolic analysts currently account for no more than 20 percent of American [workers]."

Develop Your Own Digiprise®

The corporation is dead, long live the Digiprise® – literally, the digital enterprise! The modern corporation was invented primarily to lower transaction costs in the industrial age. But with the new ways of doing business enabled by the information age, it is time to move on to a new form of business organization – the Digiprise®.

Beyond simply being a virtual corporation that outsources aspects of its business to outside suppliers, it's a place in which the network – rather than office walls – represents the enterprise. More specifically, a Digiprise® is a company that uses electronic networks and collaborative systems to form partnerships with the express intent of fulfilling a specific business opportunity or transaction. The Digiprise® moves quickly in the marketplace, creates

The Digiprise®
A Collaborative Value Network

Figure 16

dynamic collaborative solutions and can shift its shape almost at will. The Digiprise® is a process – not a specific structure.

At the completion of the transaction, while relationships between partners are maintained, the partnership disbands, and the partners seek new transactions. The Digiprise® also eliminates functional redundancies, such as payroll and distribution departments, and enables each partner to focus its attention and capital on its own core competencies. As the illustration depicts, the Digiprise has the biological structure of a dynamic amoeba not the hierarchical structure of the corporation.

Managing relationships must be a core competency of any Digiprise®. CEOs must cultivate a team of people to acquire, manage, evaluate, and disband various relationships and partnerships with outside enterprises. CEOs must empower these relationship managers to enforce the company's own standards and ethics on outside partners. If partners don't comply, that could be grounds for disbanding the partnership. But perhaps more importantly, these relationship managers must have outstanding interpersonal skills, a deep understanding of the business, and a proven ability to act and react rapidly to changing market and relationship dynamics.

In the information age, the partnerships you cultivate may well be with companies that you would otherwise think of as your worst enemies. The word that has been coined for this process is *coop-etition* (cooperating and competing with the same entities — sometimes simultaneously).

This happens regularly in the computer software industry. Since Microsoft develops the operating system software for most PCs, it is at the center of a complex network of coop-etition. Hundreds of other software companies, among them Adobe, IBM, Intuit, and Novell, compete vigorously with Microsoft when it comes to selling application software. But they must also cooperate with their industry's giant when it comes to making their applications compatible with Microsoft's operating systems. Despite the public contention in this industry, this is a system that usually works rather well. Most applications programs that you buy are nearly perfectly compatible with Microsoft's Windows operating system.

This industry may be a harbinger of things to come. Airlines that normally compete fiercely with one another in some parts of the world, for instance, are now striking deals to complement each other's service to and from some cities. United Airlines and British Airways, for instance, compete on some routes between Britain and the rest of the world, but have struck an alliance to book seats on each other's flights for customers traveling to destinations that only one of them serves. In response, Delta and Virgin Atlantic Airways struck a similar deal. A Delta customer who wants to fly from San Francisco to London will now be booked on a Virgin flight but still receive frequent flier miles on Delta.

Of course, caution is required in such partnerships. You shouldn't have to share your trade secrets, for instance, to make these kind of relationships work.

30

011110

Wire Up Collaborative Value Networks

Marketing has always been about finding the right customers for your product and creating demand among that customer base. Distribution has always been about satisfying the demand by getting your product to the proper point-of-purchase locations. Emerging information technologies allow you to blend these previously distinct activities into one smooth process – *markebution*. The idea is to be able to satisfy the demand as soon as you create it. Just think how QVC or the Home Shopping Network work. Models and pitchmen appear on TV extolling the virtues of the product of the moment. The presentation of the product creates the demand. And, of course, the 800 number flashes on the screen at all times, allowing the customer to order. Marketing and distribution, in this case, are part of the same process.

Let's examine how several companies are addressing this new way of doing business.

Many organizations are looking for ways to use the Internet to achieve this same blend. One such firm is freesheetmusic.net. You can go to their site at www.freesheetmusic.net/ and download sheet music — instant gratification. There are even services, such as The Bengal Group at www.bengal-grp.com, that offer startup assistance for entrepreneurs who want to start Internet-based drop-shipping businesses (e.g., you sell an item over the Internet for twenty dollars that a wholesaler will sell to you for ten dollars; the wholesaler delivers the goods to your customer and you pocket a ten dollar profit.)

There could be a business selling gasoline on the Internet. I go to the Web site of a major gasoline company and pull up to the virtual pump. I select the "Fill-Up" option on the pump and it asks me where my car is located. I respond with the address of the parking garage and the space number. When I go to get my car, I find the tank is now full and I pay a slight premium over retail for the gasoline. Peapod, an online grocery service, is running a similar business for Chicago-area shoppers who would rather make their selections online and have their groceries delivered.

An extranet is a virtual private network that can be used to interconnect business partners in a way that allows access to information the parties want to share, while not compromising the balance of their information systems. With the appropriate information systems security architecture, extranets can be used to effectively facilitate close communications and data exchange between business partners. They can give the partners many of the advantages they would have if they were, in fact, a single legal entity. To be successful, the partners must go beyond the technical issues and understand the extranet business relationship to be able to scope access appropriately and select the appropriate tools and defenses. Further, extranet partners should only be given access to isolated machines that contain only what they need. The partners should also establish joint, documented, information-systems security plans (including how contingencies will be handled).

Using an extranet a Fortune 100 company dramatically improved the tracking of invoice payments from the thousands of companies with which it did business by securely presenting electronic listings of complete invoices, organized by company. The companies would review all moneys owed and schedule electronic payments. The project includes an interface between the company and its bank, including the ability to securely integrate unpaid invoices into the bank's network. The extranet system included reporting, data warehousing, error correction, and logging all activity to ensure that an audit trail was maintained for the bank. The system also enabled communications with the bank's mainframe to import critical customer information.

Garden Escape, a company based in Austin, Texas, relies on an extranet to link thirty-five plant, garden-furniture, and gardening-tool suppliers to a retail site on the Internet. The entire operational side of this business is dematerialized into the extranet, leaving relationship management and product management the only major remaining aspects of the business. The gardening industry has many unusual peculiarities, such as growing seasons, the short life cycles of plants, and dependence upon weather. Rather than using the typical electronic commerce software that can define products by only a few variables, Garden Escape wanted one that could use up to ninety-four variables to describe plants, such as species, growing season, and light preferences. To meet this need, Garden Escape actually developed its own programming language to "support the gardening industry's peculiarities while meeting customers' expectations for prompt service."

Garden Escape's extranet works like this. As orders for plants or gardening supplies are placed by customers on their Internet site, they are sent directly to a database. From there, the orders are directed to the appropriate supplier and are placed in the supplier's order entry system. The orders are sent to the suppliers via e-mail requests, fax, or secure links to the supplier's database. Once the orders are processed, the supplier ships the products directly to the customer. Customer feedback is recorded on the extranet and serves as a tool for tracking customer satisfaction. In summary, Garden Escape never takes possession of the inventory, they simply make it easier for buyers and sellers to come together.

At the time of this writing, Garden Escape's extranet was already linked with 25 percent of its top thirty suppliers. To facilitate its relationship with many of its low-tech suppliers, Garden Escape has distributed Pentium PCs to link to the extranet. The company then installs the e-mail system and browser on the PCs, which are connected to Garden Escape's extranet via the Internet. Garden Escape also provides customized inventory lists and e-mail order forms to update inventory information and order confirmations. The e-mail responses feed directly into Garden Escape's electronic commerce supply chain system. This transaction automatically updates supply-level information and the status of individual orders.

The Garden Escape example illustrates the operational efficiencies of an extranet. First, the extranet automatically updates information about inventory in real time. This function is critical to a business that is distributing perishable products such as plants. In addition, the extranet provides substantial financial savings due to low labor costs and low selling and administrative costs. The only processes that necessitate human effort are at the beginning of the process when the customer makes the order online and at the end of the process when the supplier packs the merchandise in a box and ships it. By eliminating the "brick and mortar" and the paper transactions, selling and administrative costs are decreased. The end result of the extranet is reduced delivery time and improved customer satisfaction due to the direct interaction between the supplier and its customers.

What can we expect from the Digiprise® over the next ten years?

The Future of the Digiprise®

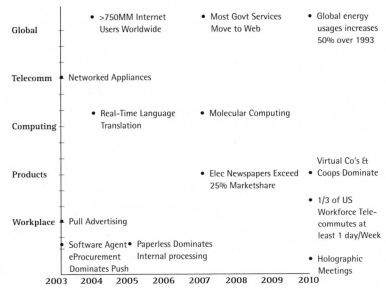

Figure 17

MASTERING DIGITAL ALCHEMY®

As a Digital Alchemist,® you should now be able to envision:

1. The culture and behaviors needed to drive your organization to achieve your new digital age goals and objectives
2. The design of a set of rewards and recognition that would promote the achievement of those desired behaviors
3. The attributes of the truly agile employee
4. Three forms of corporate knowledge that you would like to see captured and maintained in a knowledge repository
5. Two new roles in your organization and how they can be cost justified

6. Five strategic partners with whom you could begin to create a Digiprise®

7. A way to redefine your supply chain to create a collaborative value network

8. Three ways in which you can forward integrate into customer businesses

9. The impact of the Digiprise® on customer relationship management

10. The design of a transition plan to put your vision into practice

The Digital Alchemy® Process:
DELIVER

The hallmark of Digital Alchemy® is the transformation of organizations into information age gold. To complete this critical phase, the Digital Alchemist® must implement, test evaluate and correct the select strategic solutions. The crystallized vision becomes actual business process and is measured against pre-selected success metrics. Further, the Digital Alchemist® must continue looking to the horizon and visioning new solutions and business definitions. Sample best practice companies include:

- First Direct
- Pleasant Company
- Cisco Systems
- Dell Computers
- e2open

31
011111

Drive One-on-One Customer Relationship Management

Information age customers are beginning to demand higher levels of service, selection, and convenience for less time, effort, and expense. While the industrial age was an era of mass production, the information age is becoming an era of mass personalization that will ultimately end in markets of one. Emerging information technologies are making it possible for companies to deliver all of this and still be profitable.

One way to deliver a highly differentiated, customized product designed for a market-of-one yet retain some level of economies of scale is through mass customization of the product. By structuring products and services as Lego-like objects that can be bundled, unbundled, and rebundled in a variety of ways, the number of customer variations can be increased exponentially. The customer feels empowered by being able to customize the product they want, yet those choices are invisibly constrained by the architecture of the "Lego's," enabling a production economy of scale.

Another key factor is making customers feel special. This is difficult considering that in many industries, the number of direct, face-to-face customer encounters is diminishing. Consider the number of times you actually face a bank officer or teller today versus fifteen years ago. Furthermore, with increasing and global competitive threats driving the need to reduce costs, even the number of people available for customer interaction has decreased. This has resulted in a number of problems, including a lower threshold for business to be taken to a competitor as well as lost opportunities to cross-sell products and services. Mass personalization is the use of information technology to create customized markets-of-one to increase the effectiveness of those reduced customer-facing opportunities.

Midlands Bank in the United Kingdom recognized that it was not serving certain sectors of its customer base as well as it would have liked to. However, it also recognized that for a variety of reasons, it would be difficult to do so within the traditional bank. As a result, Midlands formed a subsidiary bank, First Direct. First Direct has no branch offices — no brick and mortar. It operates primarily out of a call center in Leeds, England. It has sophisticated customer and account management software that enables its well-trained staff to know all about a customer the moment the call comes in. From account balances, to demographics, to recent transactions and more, First Direct positioned itself to take maximum advantage of every customer contact. With the knowledge that a customer's child was approaching driving age, the First Direct representative could suggest a car loan at competitive rates. Or the representative might have suggestions regarding ways in which the First Direct customer could improve their money management return by investing in a CD or other instrument.

Pleasant Company, a U.S.-based doll company also employs a highly customer-intimate call center. A grandmother ordered a doll from the company using its toll-free number. The gift was wrapped and sent with a custom note. Pleasant Company not only followed up with the grandmother to ensure that the doll arrived and that her granddaughter enjoyed it, but two-and-one-half years later when she called in to order a doll for another granddaughter, they remembered the earlier transaction, thanked her for the return business, and inquired about the first granddaughter. They also noted the availability of clothes and accessories for both dolls.

Another simple example is 1-800-FLOWERS, which allows you to order flowers on the phone and package the bouquet with a personalized voice message. When the recipient gets the delivery and reads the card, there is a voice-mail number to dial for retrieving a recorded message from the sender. In Germany, the Mars Corporation holds raffles in shopping areas for a lifetime supply of pet food. When you register, you write down your pet's name, birthday, and address of your cat or dog. When your doggie's birthday rolls around, you receive a card in the mail with a sample of Mars dog food and a coupon.

On the World Wide Web, customers can be even more helpful in providing information about themselves. Companies that set up Web sites where customers review their account and billing data should also set up an area where customers can share additional pertinent information. Cyberservicing in this way helps establish a more intimate relationship with customers.

Often, you will have to pay customers for this information. But it is well worth it. MCI, for instance, recently offered millions of customers thirty minutes of free calling time if they completed a twenty-four-question survey about their use of telephone services, computers, and other media.

You may already have a substantial reservoir of data about your customers in your customer information systems, financial systems, sales systems, and elsewhere. Before purchasing third party data, consider the use of data mining and extraction software products (even if your data is in multiple systems and files) to make that customer data accessible to those who can create a competitive advantage with it.

One-on-One Customer Relationship Management

"Mrs. Williams, doesn't little Olivia need a new winter coat by now?"

Figure 18

It's not that physical products are going away. The idea is to use all the digital practices at your disposal to differentiate those physical products — to dematerialize them and focus the customer's differentiation on your knowledge and intellectual capital value-adds. You want to avoid differentiating by price, and instead wrap information around your products to distinguish them. Further, you want your customer to feel that a relationship exists between themselves and the company, generating a sense of loyalty, uncovering cross-selling opportunities, and significantly raising the threshold over which they would consider crossing to a competitor.

Precise targeting of marketing and support messages is critical to success.

32
100000

Create Effective Knowledge Repositories: Intranets and Villages

"**I**f you build it, they will come" — that's a familiar phrase from the movie *Field of Dreams*. Yet, the builders of most corporate intranets have found just the opposite to be true. Why? In addition to the obstacles piled up against knowledge sharing at most organizations, most intranets are overly techie, lack immediacy and interactivity, and do not have top management's commitment. There must be a real connection between form and substance — especially in employee communications. Using unimaginative means to ask for innovative ideas is unlikely to produce desired results.

At a major European bank, few employees were using the recently implemented intranet — designed to be a source of innovative new ideas from the bottom up. The intranet was little more than a large set of bulletin boards with topical headings. By its form alone, it clearly did not invite innovation.

The bank changed the front-end of the intranet to an exciting and interesting graphical interface that looked like a village. Buildings were created to reflect the various aspects of the bank's business. Within each building were lobby marquees that identified what discussions were taking place on each floor and then on each floor there were marquees identifying the discussions going on in each room. All employees were invited to see and experience the village. For those employees who did not have terminals or PCs on their desks, machines were made available in common areas (e.g., cafeterias, hallways, break rooms). All employees could add buildings, floors, and rooms with the one caveat that if not used within fourteen days, they would be razed. Monthly awards (e.g., premium parking for a month and special training programs) were offered to the teams who created the most useful results (metrics were defined and published by the bank).

Initially, employees visited the intranet just to see what all the talk was about. (It had been well promoted and communicated and a seed group of influential movers and shakers had been given special tours.) Usage began to grow after hours and on weekends. Then, employees began to enjoy the competition for the awards — primarily for the recognition they afforded the winners. Soon, employees indicated that their primary motivation for going to the intranet was their sense of achievement from solving problems, in many cases with people they had never met.

Similar results have been reported at National Semiconductor where a group of engineers, frustrated by finding out that someone else in the company had previously solved a difficult problem they had spent weeks on, created their own intranet. They created communities of interest that were tied to engineering topics, not organizational divisions. Anyone in the company could enroll in any community of interest. They found that this reduced development cycle times and increased job satisfaction.

In both cases, the intranets have become knowledge infrastructure, including repositories, chat rooms, discussion forums, and e-mail. They have linked people from disparate parts of their respective organizations and enabled virtual teams to form that are independent of the corporate silos and departmental turf that normally divides people. The natural extension of these systems is to eliminate the artificial boundaries created by command-and-control, hierarchical, industrial-age business models and enable self-selected teams.

Innovatively manage and disseminate knowledge throughout your organization.

Buy, Pay, and Price
in Real Time

We are already going beyond simply mirroring and improving the industrial age value chain. We are beginning to see digital networks transforming the distribution of physical products. Instead of selling TV sets, computers, and other appliances by warehousing them and collecting a small transaction fee for each purchase — like a retail catalog company — one company has created a club with a new pricing model. Consumers first pay an annual fee of $69.95 to join the club and receive an online catalog of products (though at this writing they have a special trial offer of $1.00 for the first three months). The company makes little to no money on the purchase transactions; its primary source of earnings are the membership fees. Consumers typically recoup the membership fee on their first purchase. This is a pricing model that would not be possible without digital networks.

By making information, entertainment, and other applications available to customers via the Internet or on secure CD-ROMs, organizations can create opportunities for pay-per-use software; find an application, pay for it, download it, and use it. Micropayment systems in conjunction with pay-per-use products will enable pay-per-use information, entertainment, software, music, and more. Imagine downloading maps that, based on your profile, identify the restaurants and hotels you are likely to be interested in (and providing discount coupons for them) or playing the game Doom and paying for it by the bullet.

There is clearly more to the Internet than simply being another sales channel. Anybody who has spent time surfing the Web quickly becomes astounded at how much information and entertainment is available at no charge. If the Web is such a great place to do business, why is so much stuff there available for free? What kind of business is that? More and more on the Internet is not free. Dell Computers sells more than $3 million a day on the Internet. Cisco and other companies are also doing multimillion dollar volumes daily on the Internet.

There is something larger going on in the new economy that is evolving on digital networks. Many of these free services are predicated on the notion that they will lead to two things: the sale of a higher value-added product or service and an ongoing relationship between the customer and the company. In this respect, making information available for free could be one of the most powerful practices at your disposal.

Examples of this practice are not hard to come by.

- A drug company could sponsor a free, up-to-the-minute information service about new health treatments for hospitals and doctors' offices, with the hope that it will lead to sales and loyal customers.
- At first, Netscape made its main product, its browser software, available over the Internet. Once it established market presence, it began charging for product upgrades. But then, in December 1997, with only 13 percent of revenue coming from

browser software (most comes from servers and advertising on its Web site) and Microsoft charging competitively close, they reverted to giving the browser away for free.

- Consultants are making some of their primary research reports available on the Web with the hope that they will act as sophisticated advertisements for attracting long-term clients.
- A consumer-oriented Web site, such as one from USA Today, provides sports scores and statistics for free. But USA Today can use that service to promote its online fantasy baseball, football, and basketball leagues, for which it charges a membership fee.

In most cases, but not all, you want to charge for the product or service that provides the most value-added experience to the customer.

Everyone knows that there is a time value to money. Receiving $1,000 today is often better than receiving $1,500 in six months. What many of us don't recognize, however, is that almost everything has a time value and that means there is a value to managing your business in real time.

One company reaping the benefits of real-time management over the Internet is Bay Networks Inc., a multibillion-dollar vendor of networking hardware and software based in Santa Clara, California, that was acquired by Canadian telecommunications giant Nortel Networks. "We use the following information: channel, inventory, point-of-sale information, bookings, and shipments," says Vito Palermo, vice president and corporate controller. "We crosscut that by customer, sales geography, territory, and product. How much business did we book yesterday? In Europe? What products? What margins?" Their multidimensional database allows users to make "very rapid and timely decisions," says Palermo. "Imagine having on your desktop a report: one sheet of paper. There's a set of buttons on the side: you can point and click, converting 2-D into 3-D views. I never see the [raw] data." (They use Microsoft Excel at the front end.)

With this kind of tool, almost any business could change pricing, bundling options, and offer special promotions in real time. An energy company with a sudden drop in demand could lower the price of electricity. A fast-food chain not making its daily revenue quota could offer everything at half price between 2pm and 4pm, when most people are in between meals. Such pricing and promotion practices could help smooth erratic demand cycles and increase profits. Today, organizations look at reports of what happened yesterday, last week, or last month; information age businesses must look at what is happening right now and make changes to take advantage of that knowledge.

This requires a robust and dependable way to handle high-volume, low-price transactions. Digital Equipment (Digital) has developed a payment system (Millicent) designed for payments of between one-tenth of one cent to five dollars. Most micropayment approaches on the Internet now put a minimum of ten or twenty-five cents on a transaction to cover handling costs. Digital sees their plan as having wide appeal. "We think this will capture the imaginations of people," a spokeswoman for Digital said.

Digital sees its technology being used to purchase movie previews, one song off of a CD, a horoscope, a cartoon strip, a real-time stock quote, ten seconds of play on a game, even intranet applications like metering usage of information systems or services so they can be charged to the right department. "We have the technology in pilot with Digital employees behind the firewall," the spokeswoman said. Employees use Millicent to pay for information from Reuters news service, search engine Infoseek, and Tele Danmark, Denmark's public phone and telegraph firm.

Smart cards, e-cash, and e-checks will be used to pay for online commerce. While credit cards are expected to remain the dominant payment choice for transactions greater than ten dollars, the emergence of a new micropayment market means smart card and e-money technologies will gain a growing share of the online consumer's electronic wallet for the market of online goods and services priced below ten dollars. "For now, to the extent that they buy items online, consumers are comfortable with using plastic," said Scott Smith, Group Director of the Digital Commerce Group at Jupiter

Communications. "But as new kinds of plastic emerge, like smart cards, and new types of pay-per-use services are created for the Internet, consumer behavior will change. If it's a higher-priced item, even a PC, they are likely to pay with a credit card, but if the price is low, such as for a newspaper article or game play, they will likely turn to new kinds of e-money — smart cards or electronic coins they can use on the Internet."

Today, throughout Europe, standard mobile telephones are equipped with infrared ports that can be used to make payments at vending machines — just point and click.

Coca Cola has placed sensors in some of its vending machines in Japan that can determine the outside temperature, their internal inventory, and their next resupply date. Based on this information, the machine sets pricing. When it's hot, inventory is low, and re-supply is several days away, the price goes up. Some have said all pricing will be this way within ten years.

Buy the blades, get the razor for free. What's your organization's digital age version of this story?

Participate in the Internet Digital Marketplace

Many businesses rely upon their ability to make markets by having better information than their customers. What happens when information technology levels the playing field by enabling anyone to create secondary markets through disseminating that information and creating online auctions? Not only will we see goods auctioned, but also services, knowledge, and talent.

Many companies are moving to the business-to-business (B2B) digital marketplace. One of the largest growth segments has been B2B marketplaces that are formed within a specific industry, designed to handle eProcurement.

A coal mining company could go online and offer ten tons of coal to the highest bidder of electricity. They wait and see what is offered, select the best offer, and make the exchange. This is an ex-

Table 7: Examples of B2B Internet Digital Marketplaces

Industry	Name	Representative Participants
Automobile	Covisint	Ford, GM, Daimler Chrysler
Consumer Products	Transora	Procter & Gamble, Nestle & Heinz
Chemicals	Elemica	Dow, DuPont, Shell Chemicals
Computing	e2open	IBM, Nortel Networks, Matshushita
Energy	Trade-Ranger	Total Fina Elf, BP, Amoco, Shell

ample of direct barter. But let's say that the coal mining company offered its coal for earth moving equipment, and let's say that the best offer came from a construction company that had purchased too much equipment but had a market for the coal with a local electric company. The coal mining company, construction company, and electric company each benefit by getting the best deal available for what they wanted. In fact, the only loser is the earth moving equipment manufacturer and its distributors; they are disintermediated by a technology that unites buyers and sellers with no prior knowledge of each other or their respective needs.

The Internet is an ideal place for auctioning because it brings geographically disparate markets together. Many auction businesses are forming today. In fact, auction sites, such as eBay, are one of the newest forms of life on the Internet — peer-to-peer networking. The folks at eBay facilitate auctions among peers.

Consider the way online auctions can be applied to other business areas, such as insurance companies becoming disintermediated by self-insuring pools. Those pools would secure the risk and create yet another market. Consider whether your business's products and services could serve as electronic currency (Internet barter) and become a tradable item in cyberspace. Determine how this integrates with your strategies for real-time market-making, pricing, and management.

One company, Priceline, has created a form of hybrid auctioning by offering a new way to buy airline tickets, rent hotel rooms, and rent cars. You name the price you want to pay and they try to find a major airline willing to release seats on flights where they have unsold space. Tickets can be requested up to six months in advance of departure and you are notified within one hour of your request (twenty-four hours for international) whether the seats will be available. Tickets are nonrefundable, nonchangeable, and do not earn frequent flyer miles. For leisure travelers who don't need to fly at a specific time of day or on a specific airline, this is a great new alternative. Though travel must begin in the fifty United States or Puerto Rico, you can use Priceline for tickets worldwide. And because airlines choose flights where space is available, there are no blackout dates and no advance purchase rules. Priceline intends to offer a wide range of consumer services such as new cars, home mortgages, insurance, personal computers, and more. With today's dot.com crashes, it is important to note that Priceline.com has shown its first quarterly profit (*Wall Street Journal* 8-1-2001).

Measure Your Information Age Value (GKP)

The principal value organizations will produce in the information age is based on intellectual capital and knowledge, so the importance of measuring knowledge is increasing. In the industrial age it was based on physical things you could easily see: factories, assembly lines, office equipment, and so forth. Periodically, you see office workers taking inventory of manufactured goods, factory equipment, and more mundane objects, such as desks, chairs, and boxes of staples. Yet, even though we have entered the information age, most organizations do not take stock of their information assets. In fact, information assets are often the most underutilized and underperforming resources in most companies today.

The problem, of course, lies in the fact that information isn't as easy to see as physical objects. So it's harder to count. A senior investor relations executive at Merck & Co. Inc. once noted that it is ironic that the pharmaceuticals giant must account for mundane items, such as office supplies, on its balance sheet. Merck, he said, conducts what are essentially internal inventories of its information assets. Intellectual property such as client databases, research databases for new products, and the like, are all part of that internal asset base.

There are many examples of unaccounted for information assets in almost every company. And it will probably be years before the accounting profession fully recognizes that the world has changed dramatically. But senior managers must adapt to this new reality today. Doing so will open up a whole new window on your business and enable you to create new products, services, and processes. What could be more important to a potential investor than to know the value of a company's knowledge and intellectual capital?

We should establish standard metrics for valuing our information assets. One such measure could be *Gross Knowledge Product* (GKP). While we measure economic value and growth at a macroeconomic level with Gross National Product (GNP) and Gross Domestic Product (GDP), GKP should be applied at the organizational, national, and regional levels to measure knowledge. GKP would identify knowledge importers, knowledge exporters, knowledge brokers, and knowledge surpluses and deficits. This would allow us to understand how we truly compare to others under the new rules of creating value.

A country such as Singapore may be a knowledge broker, trying to position itself to knowledge and information in the same way Switzerland has to money. A country such as the United States may be a knowledge exporter, providing critical expertise in such areas as oil and gas, manufacturing and financial services to Asia and Eastern Europe. In such cases those regions would be knowledge importers. As the information age unfolds, having a positive knowledge surplus may be more important than a positive balance of trade.

Table 8: Industrial vs. Digital-Age Values

Old Rule: Value is measured in terms of physical asset

Enabling Disruptive Cause: Dematerialization

New Rule: Value is measued in terms of knowledge & intellectual capital

Digital Alchemist's Advice: Measure & monitor your digital assets

Is your organization a knowledge importer, exporter, or broker?

36
100100

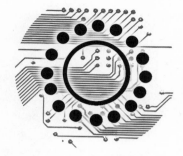

Take Advantage of Interactive Technotainment

As computing and entertainment continue to converge, computing should naturally become more entertaining. Given the choice, most consumers will opt for a product or service that's fun to use rather than one that takes a traditional, straightforward approach.

Consider the process of balancing your checkbook on the computer. Millions of consumers are doing it. But is it fun? Could it be? Perhaps Intuit should enter a joint venture with Pixar, LucasFilms, or Disney to make an entertaining version of the popular Quicken personal finance program. Maybe it can become like an animated game. If your checking account reconciles perfectly at the end of the month, perhaps an animated creature can appear on your screen. Perhaps you can set a monthly savings objective at the beginning of the year. When you reach your goal, you could score points just like in a video game.

Online banking should be fun. Doing your taxes electronically should be fun. Ordering fast-food at a restaurant should be fun (and it will be if the self-service video terminals that PepsiCo is introducing at some Taco Bells catch on.) Even a company's internal procurement interface should be lively. Web sites centered around shopping and customer service should also be fun. Integrating entertainment into mundane tasks should noticeably increase the number of transactions among customers, suppliers, and employees.

Microsoft launched a career center in mid-1996 designed to encourage employees to search within Microsoft when they wanted a new job. To drive participation they made it fun. It has a jungle theme ("It's a jungle out there"). Without being condescending or overly silly, there are dozens of boring activities on the computer that can be transformed into fun ones — ones customers will come back to over and over again.

MASTERING DIGITAL ALCHEMY®

As a Digital Alchemist®, you should now be able to envision:
1. At least one way in which one of your products can be unbundled to enable customers to select their own mass-customized version
2. An application of cyberservicing in your business
3. The scripting and development of a personalized telesales and teleservice program
4. Three topics that your organization could build intranet knowledge communities around and their benefits
5. How your company might be reorganized using virtual, self-directed teams rather than traditional, stove-pipe departments
6. Criteria with which you could apply dynamic pricing
7. How you can use online auctions to reduce excess inventory
8. Five potential partners who might partner with you to pur-

chase supplies online

9. At least one way you could measure the value of your firm's intellectual assets, other than traditional patent and copyright appraisal

10. A way to make doing business with your organization entertaining

The Digital Alchemy® Process:
GOING FORWARD

The arrival of the information age may be the most profound change mankind has ever faced. While Guten-
berg's printing press brought books to the common man,
interactive information technologies such as the Internet
are making the common man a publisher. The number
of ideas that will be generated and the velocity of

those ideas will be immense and the results unpredictable. We may
see the end of the nation-state as we know it today and the corporation, too. Without the physical limitations that we have had in
the past, we are free to dream and make those dreams real.

You must now maintain, update, and articulate a compelling vision for your organization's future — all the while strategically using
information technology to accelerate the implementation of that vision. The Thirty-six Digital Alchemy® Strategies are a means to that
end. If you have not implemented some of these practices already,
look back over the four categories of practices and decide which
makes sense for your company to implement first. If you are well
on your way, decide which category you need to implement next.
And as you decide which practices to act upon today, remember what
Einstein said: "In the middle of difficulty lies opportunity."

You don't have to be Einstein to realize that companies making
the leap into the information age are facing intense difficulty cop-
ing with entirely new ways of doing things. Yet taking advantage
of the opportunities at hand is a must. Proactive leadership by senior management is perhaps *the* critical success factor.

Recent events have strongly underlined the need for real-time
management using scenario-based thinking. The tragic bombing of
the World Trade Center in New York, a drastic downturn in the U.S.
and global economies, and the effects these events have had on business (e.g., less business travel, increased tele- and video-conferencing,
higher unemployment, reduced consumer spending, etc.), have led
to a business environment that few would have forecast. Funda-
mentally, good strategic thinking is not about predicting the future,
it is about identifying the plausible futures and then planning
ahead for their eventualities.

Perhaps the five most important challenges the Digital Al-
chemist® faces today are these:

1. Focus on strategic *thinking*, not traditional strategic planning.
   Move to ready — aim — steer, real-time business management.
2. Operate in Web-time with a customer-centric perspective.
   Constantly look for opportunities to forward integrate and

offer new value to your customers through new products, services, and processes. Make your organization essential to do business with.

3. Culture, organizational behavior, and change management cannot be underestimated. Communicate often and effectively, take ownership within the business, not in shared services such as information technology, and start early.

4. Reinvent your supply chain. Identify opportunities to reduce cycle times and costs, to implement e-procurement, and to develop better strategic relationships with your suppliers.

5. Constantly challenge your business models. With competitive advantage being commoditized at an accelerating rate, if you do not challenge your business models you can count on your competitors doing it for you and then redefining the rules of competition.

Finally, remember the words of Harry Truman: "Progress occurs when courageous, skillful leaders seize the opportunity to change things for the better." This is every Digital Alchemist®'s ongoing challenge.

Section Three
Appendices

RESOURCES
AND TOOLS

Appendix 1

Web Sites of Interest to Digital Alchemists®

Business-to-Business Examples

www.e-fin.com
   Automobile credit services for dealers, financial institutions, and consumers

www.verticalnet.com
   Twenty different B2B industry sites

www.converge.com
   Electronic components, computer and networking products

www.vitra.com
European high quality office furniture

www.lundstromarch.com
Lundstrom & Associates architectural firm

www.photodisc.com
Photographic and digital imagery

www.northwesternmutual.com
Small business services, risk management

www.hmstore.com
Herman Miller office furniture

www.build.net
Commercial/home construction manufacturers/distributors/builders

www.cisco.com
Configuration and ordering of networking equipment

www.dell.com
Configuration and ordering of personal computers

www.milpro.com
Cutting and grinding tools, metalworking fluids

www.metalsite.com
Surplus steel

www.polymerland.com
Supplies to the plastics producer market

Business-to-Consumer Examples

www.netgrocer.com
Grocery and perishable food items

www.justballs.com
Athletic equipment involving balls

www.nick.com
Nickelodeon games, toys, merchandise

www.pseudo.com
Real-time TV network, music, fashion

www.fool.com
Motley Fool financial and investment advice and books

www.tuneup.com
Online performance and tuning of personal computers

www.wine.com
Wine buying

www.nike.com
Footwear and apparel

www. planetRx.com
OTC drugs and personal care products

www.autobytel.com
Automotive purchasing

www.improvenet.com
Home improvement

www.finet.com
Mortgage services

www.cdnow.com
Music and video purchasing

www.witcapital.com
IPO offerings

www.e-trade.com
Brokerage services

Government-to-Constituent Examples

www.efile.gov
IRS tax filing

www.stamps.com
US Postal Service approved online stamp vendor

www.hq.nasa.gov/office/procurement
NASA Office of Procurement

www.ec.fed.gov
GSA's eCommerce site; GSA Advantage

www.seniors.gov/
Access America for Seniors — a multi-governmental portal for senior citizens linking fifteen agencies, including the IRS, FCC, GSA, HCFA, VA, State, and SSA

Industry Information

www.companysleuth.com
CompanySleuth

www.cnet.com
  CNET

www.foresight.org/
  Foresight Institute

www.redherring.com/
  Red Herring

www.santafe.edu
  Santa Fe Institute

www.wired.com
  Wired

www.zdnet.com
  ZDNet

Research

www.forrester.com
  Forrester

www.jup.com
  Jupiter

www.nua.ie/surveys
  NUA

Marketing

www.cyberatlas.com
  Cyberatlas

www.emarketer.com
eMarketer

Business News

www.bbb.com.uk
BBC

www.businessweek.com
Business Week

www.fortune.com
Fortune

www.hbsp.harvard.edu/products/hbr
Harvard Business Review

Appendix 2

Glossary

Applets
Tiny computer programs that can be downloaded from the Web and executed without the permanent installation of specialized software on your computer. *See also* Plug-ins.

ASP (Application Service Provider)
A firm that provides specific services (e.g., billing, payroll) via electronic connection.

Banner
A graphic image on a Web site used to promote another Web site that can be accessed by clicking on the graphic.

BBS (Bulletin Board System)
An online forum for users to read and post information; a public discussion area.

BPS (Bits per second)
The speed at which information is transmitted (usually via a modem.)

Browser
Computer program that makes it possible to navigate Web pages, viewing text and graphics. Netscape and Microsoft Internet Explorer are two widely used browsers.

Chat
A method of online communication that allows users to communicate in real time. Information typed on one person's computer is immediately displayed on another's computer.

Compression
Reducing the size of a file in order to reduce transmission time.

Cookies
A text file planted by a Web site on a user's computer so that when the user returns to the site, it will have information about the user's preferences.

Data Mining
Analyzing a collection of data to identify meaningful patterns (e.g., red widgets are purchased by 57 percent of the male customers who buy widgets online).

Dematerialization
The increased focus on knowledge and intellectual capital, rather than merely physical capital and size, to create value.

Dial-up
To connect your computer to another computer by calling it up via modem.

Digiprise®
A digital enterprise in which suppliers, partners, customers, and your organization are linked in a collaborative value network.

DNS (Domain Name Server)
A computer that matches domain names to numeric IP addresses, making them easier to locate.

Download
To receive a file from another computer into your computer.

FAQ (Frequently Asked Questions)
Answers to common questions that can be accessed at any time.

Frames
A Web page layout technique that divides the page into several smaller pages on one screen. Not all Web browsers support frames.

FTP (File Transfer Protocol)
A method of transferring files from one computer to another. This method is especially useful for transferring files from a computer to a Web site.

GIF
One format for displaying graphics on Web pages.

Home Page
The first page on a Web site from which other pages at the site can be accessed.

Hypertext Markup Language (HTML)
A coding standard that specifies how Web pages should be displayed by browsers.

http:// (Hypertext Transfer Protocol)
The standard prefix for most addresses on the Web. *See also* URL.

Hypertext Links
Highlighted or underlined words or images on a Web page that link that page to other related pages or files. Navigation is accomplished by clicking a mouse on the hypertext link.

Internet
A worldwide network of computer networks that are connected to each other, providing file transfer, remote login, e-mail, news, and other services.

Internet Service Provider (ISP)
Any organization that provides direct access to the Internet.

Java
A programming language that accommodates applets into Web page design.

JPEG
A format used to display graphics on Web pages.

Meta Tags
Key words used in the HTML code of a Web site that is accessed by search engines to find a particular Web site.

MIME (Multipurpose Internet Mail Extension)
Allows the transmission of text, graphics, video, and sound across the Internet as an attachment to an e-mail message.

Modem
A device that allows a computer to connect to the Internet over conventional phone lines. Modem speeds are expressed in bits per second (bps).

Online
Being connected to the Internet.

Plug-ins
Small software accessories that work in conjunction with a Web browser to give it added capabilities, such as the ability to play sounds or video. Unlike applets, plug-ins must be installed on your computer in advance and configured to work with your browser.

Portal
A gateway Web site that provides access to other Web sites. Yahoo.com is a popular portal.

Search Engine
One of several services on the Web designed to help users locate Web sites on specific subjects. The user types in a search word or phrase and is given a range of sites to choose from. Two popular search engines that can search the entire Web are Google (http://www.google.com) and AltaVista (http://www.altavista.com).

Server
A machine that makes services available on a network. A file server enables others to access files, while a Web server is the computer system that makes its Web pages available to others through the HTTP protocol.

T/1 or T/3 lines
High-speed network links that greatly reduce the time users wait for Web pages to download.

URL (Universal Resource Locator)
The address of a Web page. Most URLs begin with the prefix http://.

Virtual Reality
The use of a computer to closely simulate real life situations (e.g., turning 2-dimensional blueprints into a 3-dimensional walk-through of a model home online).

World Wide Web (WWW)
Multimedia pages and resources that reside on the Internet, which are woven together through the use of hypertext links.

Appendix 3

Index

Page numbers followed by *t* and *f* refer
to tables and figures respectively.

A

Access America for Seniors, Web
    site, 168
Accountability, centralization and,
    10
Action stimulators, 15
    for Align step, 63–64
    for Deliver step, 154–155
    for Innovate step, 103–104
    for Understand step, 63
Adaptec, Inc., 108
Addressable devices, 74–75
Adobe, Inc., 125
Advertising. *See also* Marketing
on Internet, 85–87

payment structure for,
    86–87
narrowcasting and, 47–48
"The Age of Social Transforma-
    tion" (Drucker), 120
Agility, as valued skill, 4, 113–114,
    117
Agrarian economy, characteristics
    of, 5, 5*t*
Airline industry, coopetition in,
    125
Alchemists, characteristics of, xxii,
    15–16. *See also* Digital Al-
    chemist(s)®
Alchemy glyphs, meaning of, xi

Align step, xxvi, 15*f*, 18*f*
  action stimulators for, 63–64
  activities in, 20–21
  best practice companies, 108
  goal of, 20, 107–108
  Thirty-six Digital Alchemy®
    Strategies in, 109–130
Allegory, in innovative thinking,
  19–20
America in the New Economy
  (Carnevale), 113
America Online, 47, 54
American Airlines, 80, 94–95
American Greetings, Inc., 43
Ameritrade, 9
Analogy, in innovative thinking,
  19–20
Applets, definition of, 171
Appliances, IP (Internet protocol)
  addresses in, 74–75
Application Service Provider
  (ASP), definition of, 171
Aptitude profile for Digital Al-
  chemists®, 15, 24–26
The Art of War (Sun Zi), 14
Arvida Realty, 57
ASP (Application Service
  Provider), definition of, 171
Atlantic Monthly, 120
AT&T, 54, 97*f*
Auctions, on Internet, 147–149
Auto-By-Tel, 32, 49–50
Automobiles
  shopping for, on Internet,
    49–50
  smart technology in, 77
Avis, 58

B
B2B (business-to-business) mar-
ketplace, on Internet,
  147–148, 148*t*, 165–166
Banking, online, 44, 154
Banners, 85–86
  definition of, 171
Barter, on Internet, 147–148
Bay Networks Inc., 144
BBC, 170
BBS (Bulletin Board System), defi-
  nition of, 172
Bengal Group, 127
Bits per second (BPS), definition
  of, 172
Boolean search engines, 90
Bose Corporation, 67, 80
Boston Beer Company, 108
BPS (bits per second), definition
  of, 172
Brand name
  vs. mindshare, 96
  value of, 96–98, 97*f*
Breakthrough thinking, techniques
  for, 19–20
British Airways, 125
British Gas, 9
British Petroleum, 10
Broadband communication
  impact of, 34, 34*t*
  leveraging of, 75
Browser, definition of, 172
Bulletin Board System (BBS), defi-
  nition of, 172
Business
  current state of knowledge in,
    xxi–xxii
  focus of
    customers as, 16, 158–159
    redefining, 38–40
  global, characteristics of, 59–60
  goals of, reevaluating, 18

in information age, 3–7, 5*t*,
31–32
innovation in, importance of,
7–8, 159
on Internet. *See also Digiprise®*
business-to-business,
147–148, 148*t*,
165–166
pay-per-use products, 143,
145–146
as requirement in information age, 42–43
new roles in, 120–122
redefining, need for, 8–12, 11*f*,
38–40, 65–66
strategy for. *See* Strategy
Business news, Web sites on, 170
Business-to-business (B2B) marketplace, on Internet,
147–148, 148*t*, 165–166
Business-to-consumer Web sites,
167–168
Business Week, 18–19, 170
Byran, John, 97

C
Career development skills, value
of, 117
Carnevale, Anthony, 113
Cellular phones
electronic payments and, 146
history of, 7
opportunities opened by, 75
Cendant Corporation, 58
Centralization
and accountability, 10
in information age, 32
Century 21 Realtors, 58
CEOs (chief executive officers),
support from, 16, 23–24

Change
adaptability to, as valued skill,
4, 113–114, 117
anticipation of, 4, 68–73
competition as driver of, 7,
21–22
embracing, 11–12
employee training and,
117–119
management of, corporate cul-
ture and, 159
rapid pace of, 3–4, 7
Channels
management of, 66, 66*f*
new, business strategy and, 11*f*
Charles Schwab, Inc., 55
Chat, definition of, 172
Chevrolet Nova, 60
Chief executive officers. *See* CEOs
Chrysler Corp., 86
Cisco, 108
Classification, in data mining, 46
Click-through ads, 85–86
Clickstreams, data mining of, 46
Clustering, in data mining, 46
CNET, 169
Coca Cola Corporation, 146
Cochrane, Peter, xxi–xxiv
Coldwell Banker, 58
Collaborative value networks,
126–130
Collaborative virtual workspaces
advantages of, 102–103
applications for, 101–102
building of, 102
future directions in, 103
Collegiality, value of, 115
Communication(s)
broadband
impact of, 34, 34*t*

leveraging of, 75
narrowcasting
    advertising and, 47–48
    impact of, 34, 34t
wireless
    impact of, 34, 34t
    leveraging of, 74–75
    privacy and, 34
Communication skills, value of, 114
Communities, on Internet, 51–52
Competition
    coopetition in, 125
    as driver of change, 7, 21–22
    in global marketplace
        company size and, 56–58
        glocalizing and, 59–60
        niching vs. consolidation in,
            56–58
    in information age, 8–10
    monitoring, in rapidly chang-
        ing environment, 66
Compression, definition of, 172
Computer(s)
    desktop, personalized, 81–82
    entertainment value of,
        153–154
    literacy skills in, value of, 116
    ubiquity of, 4
Computer software industry,
    coopetition in, 125
ConceptLabs, xxi
Conflict resolution strategy, in in-
    formation age, 11f
Consolidation, in global market-
    place, 56–58
Consumer clubs, 142
Content management, XML and,
    92, 92f
Content tagging, for electronic
    searches, 91–92, 91t

Convenience, consumer preference
    for, 113. See also One-stop
    shopping
Cookies
    definition of, 172
    and privacy, 48
Coopers & Lybrand, 42
Coopetition, 125
Corporate Alchemy®, e-mail ad-
    dress of, 26
Corporate culture, change man-
    agement and, 159
Critical drivers of technology-en-
    abled business strategy,
    33–35
Cultural diversity, global business
    and, 59
Culture sensitivity, as valued skill,
    116
Customer(s)
    building relationship with
        via customer service, 80–82
        via feedback, 53–55
        via free Internet products/
            services, 143–144
        via personalized service,
            81–82, 136–138
    feedback from
        in information age, 32
        Internet as tool for, 53–55
        and personalized service,
            137–138
    as focus of business, 16,
        158–159
    information on. See also Data
        mining; Micromarket
        segmentation
    requesting, 137
    on Internet

building relationship with, 143–144

desires and expectations of. *See* Cyberpsychographics

interacting with, 32, 53–55

tracking of, 55

and one-stop shopping, 49–50, 95

personalizing contact with, 81–82, 135–138

preferences of, in information age, 113, 135–136

retaining
  product differentiation and, 138
  value of, 53–55
  segmentation of. *See* Micromarket segmentation
  service expectations of, 41–44, 44*t*

Customer service
  building relationships with, 80–82
  customer expectations for, 41–44, 44*t*
  goals of, 136
  importance of, 53–55
  one-on-one, in information age, 81–82, 135–138, 138*f*
  product differentiation and, 138
  self-service and, 41–44

Customization, consumer preference for, 113

Cyberatlas, 169

Cyberpsychographics
  definition of, 14, 41
  importance of understanding, 32
  overview of, 41–44, 44*t*

Cybrarian, 121

D

Data, worker's inability to use, 121

Data mining
  definition of, 45, 172
  impact of, 34, 34*t*
  in micromarket segmentation, 45–48
  in personalizing of service, 137
  and privacy, 48
  tools, sources of, 46

Data warehouse architectures, data mining and, 46

Databases
  linking to Web sites, 91
  and real time pricing, 144–145
  searches on
    limitations of, 90–91
    next-generation, 92
    tagging content for, 91–92, 91*t*

Davidow, Bill, 96

Deliver step, xxvi, 15*f*, 18*f*
  action stimulators for, 154–155
  activities in, 21–22
  goal of, 21, 133–134
  Thirty-six Digital Alchemy® Strategies in, 135–154

Dell Computers, 143

Delta Airlines, 125

Dematerialization
  definition of, 7, 172
  focusing on, 18
  in information age, 11*f*
  of people, 101–103
  of products and services, 6–8

Desktop, of computer, personalized, 81–82

Dial-up, definition of, 173

Differentiation of products, 138

Digiprise®
  characteristics of, 123–125, 124*f*
  collaborative value networks and, 126–130
  definition of, 15, 173
  future of, 130*f*
  in information age, 11*f*
Digital age. *See* Information age
Digital Alchemist(s)®
  aptitude profile test for, 15, 24–26
  institutional support for, 16, 20–21, 23–24, 71
  role of, 6–7
  skills required by, 11–12, 15–16, 19–20, 23–24
The Digital Alchemist® (Marcus)
  purpose of, xxv
  structure of, xxv–xxvi
Digital Alchemy® practices. *See* Innovation(s)
Digital Alchemy® process
  advantages of, xxvii, 11
  definition of, x
  feedback loops in, 17, 18*f*, 21
  steps in, xxvi, 17–22. *See also individual steps* (Understand; Innovate; Align; Deliver)
Digital Alchemy® Strategies. *See* Thirty-six Digital Alchemy® Strategies
Digital Equipment, 145
Directory services on Web, 79–80
DirecTV, 75
Disney Corp., 47
Dispute resolution skills, value of, 115–116

Distribution
  changes, opportunities in, 86
  and marketing, mingling of, 126–127
DNS (Domain Name Server), definition of, 173
Download, definition of, 173
Drawing/visualization, in breakthrough thinking, 19
Drop-shipping businesses, 127
Drucker, Peter, 120

E
e-communities, 51–52
e-mail, customer expectations for, 42
e-money, 145–146
eBay, 148
Economies of knowledge, 10–12
Economies of scale, as industrial age concept, 10
Economy
  agrarian, characteristics of, 5, 5*t*
  downturn in, effects of, 158
  industrial
    characteristics of, 5, 5*t*
    freeing one's mind from, 18
    valuation in, 152*t*
  in information age. *See* Information age
Education
  continual, importance of, 117–119
  self-directed, 119
Einstein, Albert, 158
Electric power, history of, 7
eMarketer, 170
Embedded intelligence. *See* Smart technology
Employers, skills needed by, 113–117

Employment patterns, changes in, 112–113
Energy industry, in information age, 8–9
Entertainment
  computing as, 153–154
  pay-per-use, 143, 145–146
eProcurement, 147–148, 148*t*
ERA Inc., 58
Ernie, 99–100
Ernst & Young, 67, 100
ESPNET Sports Zone, 46–47
Everett, Rich, 86
eXtensible Markup Language. *See* XML
Extranet, as collaborative value network, 127–129

F
Factories and plants, in information age, 6, 112
Family Planet, 47
FAQ (Frequently Asked Questions), definition of, 173
Fax machines, history of, 7
Federal Express, 44, 86, 108, 119
Feedback, from customers
  in information age, 32
  Internet as tool for, 53–55
  and personalized service, 137–138
Feedback loops, in Digital Alchemy® process, 17, 18*f*, 21
Field of Dreams (film), 139
File Transfer Protocol (FTP), definition of, 173
First Direct (U.K.), 32, 136
5 Ps, 102
Focus groups, *vs.* Internet feedback, 54

Focus of business
  customers as, 16, 158–159
  redefining, 38–40
Foresight Institute, 169
Forrester, 169
Fortune magazine, 18–19, 170
Frames, definition of, 173
Frequently Asked Questions (FAQ), definition of, 173
FTP (File Transfer Protocol), definition of, 173
Future
  planning for, 158
  predicting
    innovation and, 21
    methods for, 17–18
    need for, 13
    possibility of, xxi–xxii
  vision for
    implementation of, 21–22
    evaluating needs for, 20–21
    importance of, 13, 158

G
Garden Escape, 128–129
Gasoline, selling on Internet, 127
Gatekeepers, software agents and, 94–95
Gates, Bill, 113–114
General Electric Corp., 55, 108
General Motors (GM), 60
GIF, definition of, 173
GKP (Gross Knowledge Product), 151
Global business, characteristics of, 59–60
Global marketplace
  company size and, 56–58
  glocalizing and, 59–60

niching *vs.* consolidation in, 56–58
Global positioning system (GPS), 75
Glocalizing, 59–60
GM (General Motors), 60
Goals and objectives, reevaluating, 18. *See also* Vision
Google, 66
Government-to-constituent Web sites, 168
GPS (Global positioning system), 75
Graphics, online, downloading of, 91*t*
Grocery services, online, 127
Gross Knowledge Product (GKP), 151
Group skills, value of, 115
GSA Web site, 168

H
Hallmark, Inc., 43
Harley Davidson, Inc., 102–103
Harvard Business Review, 102, 170
Herman Miller, Inc., Web site, 166
Hewlett-Packard Corp., 67
High-speed computing, impact of, 33, 34*t*
Home Page, definition of, 173
Home Shopping Network, 126
Household devices, addressable, 74–75
HTML (Hypertext Markup Language), definition of, 174
http:// (Hypertext Transfer Protocol), definition of, 174
Hypertext links, definition of, 174

I
IBM Corp., 125

Implementation of vision, 21–22
evaluating needs for, 20–21
Industrial economy
characteristics of, 5, 5*t*
freeing one's mind from, 18
valuation in, 152*t*
Industry information Web sites, 168–169
Infogate.com, 81–82
Infonomics
definition of, 14
in information age, 11*f*
Information. *See also* Knowledge
about information, leveraging of, 79–80, 100
as commodity, 79–80
on customers. *See also* Data mining; Micromarket segmentation
requesting, 137
differentiation of products and, 138
sharing
importance of, 110–111
incentives for, 109–110
ubiquity of, and competitive markets, 36–37, 66, 147
as value-added product, 8–9
Information age
business in, 3–7, 5*t*, 31–32
need to redefine, 8–12, 11*f*
challenges of, 158–159
characteristics of, xxvi, 6
competition in, 8–10
impact of, 157–158
models of thinking in, 10–11
new roles in, 120–122
opportunities in, 12
reward structures in, 109–111
skills needed in, 112–117

transparency of markets in,
36–37, 66, 147
valuation in, 150–151, 152*t*
Information intermediaries, information age and, 9–10, 66
InfoSeek, 79–80
Innovate step, xxvi, 15*f*, 18*f*
action stimulators for, 103–104
activities in, 19–20
best practice companies, 67
goal of, 19, 65–67
Thirty-six Digital Alchemy®
Strategies in, 65–103
Innovation(s)
in business models, importance
of, 7–8, 159
business strategy and, 11*f*
development of, 21–22
forecasting impact of, 21
identifying, approaches for,
68–73
importance of, 7–8
resistance to, 71–72
testing and evaluation of, 21
value of, importance of measuring, 21
Innovation pyramid exercise, 70,
70*f*
Institutional support
for Digital Alchemist®, 16,
23–24
for implementation of vision,
20–21
for SAGE program, 71
Insurance industry, in information
age, 10
Intel Corp., 62, 67
Intellectual capital. *See* Knowledge
Intelligence, embedded. *See* Smart
technology

IntelliMarketing, definition of, 15
Interactive marketing, 85–87
characteristics of, 32
Interfaces, user-friendly, advantages of, 61–62
Intermediaries, in information age,
9–10, 66
Internet. *See also entries under*
Online; World Wide Web
addressable devices and, 74–75
advertising on, 85–87
payment structure for,
86–87
auctions on, 147–149
barter on, 147–148
and brand name, value of,
96–98, 97*f*
business on. *See also* Digiprise®
business-to-business,
147–148, 148*t*, 165–166
pay-per-use products, 143,
145–146
as requirement in information age, 42–43
customers on
building relationship with,
143–144
desires and expectations of.
See Cyberpsycho-
graphics
interacting with, 32, 53–55
tracking of, 55
definition of, 174
e-communities on, 51–52
free products/services on,
143–144
intermediaries on, 66
markebution on, 127
Micromarket segmentation and,
53–55

pay-per-use products on, 143,
145–146
searches on
limitations of, 90–91
next-generation, 92
tagging content for, 91–92, 91*t*
senior citizens and, 43
shopping on, one-stop, 49–50, 95
in trend analysis, 18–19
volume of use, 42, 82*f*
Internet protocol (IP) addresses, in
appliances, 74–75
Internet Service Provider (ISP),
definition of, 174
Intranets
as knowledge repositories,
140–141
resistance to, 139–140
Intuit Corp., 125, 153
IP (Internet protocol) addresses, in
appliances, 74–75
IRS Web site, 168
Isadra, Inc., 108
ISP (Internet Service Provider),
definition of, 174

J
Java, definition of, 174
JPEG, definition of, 174
Jupiter Communications,
145–146, 169

K
Kanter, Rosabeth Moss, 102
Keyword searches
limitations of, 90–91
tagging content for, 91–92, 91*t*
KFC (Kentucky Fried Chicken),
Inc., 58, 60
Knowledge. *See also* Information

economies of, 10–12
increased value of, 6
international trade in, 151
management of, learning curve
and, 118–119
sharing of, intranets and,
140–141
valuation of, 150–151, 152*t*
Knowledge acquirer, 121
Knowledge repositories, 139–141
Knowledge representer, 121
Knowledge workers
business life of, 118
growth in, 120
role of, 120–122
shortage of, 121–122

L
Landmarks of Tomorrow (Drucker),
120
Leaders, in global business, 59–60
Learning
continual, importance of,
117–119
self-directed, 119
Learning curve, knowledge man-
agement and, 118–119
Levi's, 96
Lexus, 32, 97
Lexus Centre of Performing Arts, 97
Librarian, digital (cybrarian), 121
Lifelong learning, importance of,
117–119
Listening skills, value of, 115
Lundstrom & Associates, Web site,
166

M
Management, flattening of, 112

Marcus, Eric
  biography of, xxii–xxiii,
    179–181
  e-mail address, 26
Markebution, definition of,
  126–127
Market(s). *See also* Micromarket
    segmentation
  B2B (business-to-business), on
    Internet, 147–148, 148*t*,
    165–166
  global
    company size and, 56–58
    glocalizing and, 59–60
    niching *vs.* consolidation in,
      56–58
  information transparency in,
    36–37, 66, 147
  trends in, analysis of, 18–19
  and ubiquity of information,
    impact of, 36–37, 66, 147
Marketing. *See also* Advertising
  brand names and, 96–98, 97*f*
  and distribution, mingling of,
    126–127
  interactive, 85–87
    characteristics of, 32
    on Internet, 85–87
    narrowcasting and, 47–48
    virtual reality interfaces and,
      62, 88–89
  Web sites on, 169–170
Marriott Corporation, 32
Marriott Vacation Club Interna-
    tional, 47–48
Mars Corporation, 137
Mass customization, 135–138
Mass mailings, *vs.* targeted mar-
    keting, 47–48
Mass personalization, 135–138

McCaw Cellular, 54
MCI Corporation, 136
Medtronic, Inc., 67
MEMS (microelectromechanical
    sensors), 77
Merck & Co., 32, 150–151
Mergers and acquisitions, impact
    of, 56–58
Merrill, Charles, 20
Meta tags, definition of, 174
Metaphor, in innovative thinking,
    19–20
MetroMail, 45–46
Microelectromechanical sensors
    (MEMS), 77
Micromarket segmentation
  advantages of, 17–18, 45–48
  Internet as tool for, 53–55
Micropayment systems, 145–146
Microsoft Corporation, 113–114,
    154
Microsoft Network, 47, 54
Middle management, shrinking of,
    112
Midlands Bank, 136
Millicent payment system, 145
MIME (Multipurpose Internet Mail
    Extension), definition of, 174
Mindshare, *vs.* brand, 96
MIT Media Lab, 43, 77
Modem, definition of, 175
Moore, Gordon, 62
Moore's Law, 62
Motley Fool, Web site, 167
Mr. Showbiz, Web site, 47
Multipurpose Internet Mail Exten-
    sion (MIME), definition of,
    174
Music, pay-per-use, 143, 145–146

N

Nan Chi Shi, 14
Narrowcasting
  and advertising, 47–48
  impact of, 34, 34t
NASA Web site, 168
National semiconductor, 108
Negroponte, Nicholas, 43, 77
net.Genesis, 55
Netscape, 143–144
Niche companies, opportunities in
  global marketplace, 56–58
Nike Corp., 108, 167
Nonlinear thinking, techniques
  for, 19–20
Nortel Networks, 144
Novell Corp., 125
NUA, 169

O

OLAP (On-Line Analytical Pro-
  cessing), 46
1-800-FLOWERS, 136–137
One-on-one customer service, in
  information age, 81–82,
  135–138, 138f
One-stop shopping
  advantages of, 49–50
  software agents and, 95
Online, definition of, 175
Online banking, 44, 154
Online graphics, downloading of,
  91t
Online grocery services, 127
Opportunities, identifying, ap-
  proaches for, 68–73
Oracle, 108
Organic Online, Inc., 97
Outside Online, 47

P

Pacemakers, 99
Palermo, Vito, 144
Parker Pen, Inc., 60
Pay-per-use products, on Internet,
  143, 145–146
PCS (personal communication sys-
  tems), 75
Peapod, Inc., 127
People, dematerialization of,
  101–103
PeopleSoft, Inc., 43–44
Pepsi Co., 60, 154
Personal communication systems
  (PCS), 75
Personalization
  of customer contacts, 81–82,
  135–138
  in information age strategy, 11f
  of Web sites, 84
Pfizer Corp., 55
Phagocytosis, 71–72
Phagonovoideasis, 71–72
Phantom supercompetitor exer-
  cise, 68–69
PHH Mortgage, 58
Pleasant Company, 136–137
Plug-ins, definition of, 175
PointCast, 81
Portal, definition of, 175
Practices, innovative. See Innova-
  tion(s)
Presley Homes, 32, 88
Price, differentiation of products
  and, 138
PriceLine, 32, 148–149
Pricing
  real-time, 11f, 144–145
  in transparent markets, 36–37,
  66, 147

Prioritizing of projects, 21
Privacy
   cookies and, 48
   data mining and, 48
   wireless technology and, 34
Problem solving skills, value of, 114
Product(s)
   dematerialization of, 6–8
   differentiation of, 138
   pricing of
      in real-time, 11*f*, 144–145
      in transparent markets,
         36–37, 66, 147
   servicizing of, 99–100
Productizing of services, 99–100
Prudential Florida, 57

Q
Quicken, 153
QVC, 86, 126

R
R. L. Polk, 46
Ragu, 97–98
Ready-fire-steer model, 11*f*,
   158–159
Real-time management
   benefits of, 144–145
   need for, 158–159
Red Herring, 96, 169
Reed, David, 102
Reich, Robert, 121–122
Reinventing the wheel, avoiding,
   110–111
Reports, real-time, 144–145
Republishing content on Web, 91*t*,
   92, 92*f*
Research, Web sites on, 169
Results, measurement of, 21
Reward structures

in information age, 109–111
   intranet use and, 140
Roles, in information age, 120–122

S
Sabre system, 80
SAGE (Scenario-based Accelerated
   Gameplanning Environ-
   ment), 70–73, 72*f*
Santa Fe Institute, 169
Saturn car company, 97
Scenario-based Accelerated Game-
   planning Environment
   (SAGE), 70–73, 72*f*
Science, lack of, in business,
   xxi–xxii
Sculley, John, 53
Search engines
   definition of, 175
   limitations of, 90–91
   next-generation, 92
   tagging content for, 91–92, 91*t*
Sears, 86
Self-directed learning, 119
Self-directed work teams, 112
Self-service, desirability of, 43
Senior citizens, and Internet, 43
September 11th attack, impact of,
   158
Server, definition of, 175
Service. *See* Customer service
Services
   dematerialization of, 6–8
   productizing of, 99–100
Servicizing of products, 99–100
"Share-aware" software, 103
Shopping, one-stop, advantages
   of, 49–50
Singapore, 151
Skills

desirable, in information age,
112–117
rapid aging of, 4
updating, importance of,
117–119
Smart cards, 145–146
Smart hits, 47
Smart technology
in houses, 74–75
new value in, 4
as profit opportunity, 76–78,
77f
in real-time pricing, 146
Smith, Adam, 121
Smith, Scott, 145–146
Software, pay-per-use, 143,
145–146
Software agents
blocking of, 95
definition of, 94
uses of, 94–95, 95t
Southern Chi dynasty, 14
Southwest Airlines, 57
Speech-based interfaces, 61–62,
82f
St. Joe Paper Co., 57
Starwave Corporation, 32, 46–47
Stockbrokers, in information age,
9–10
Strategic thinking, goal of, 158
Strategy
development of, 21–22
grassroots understanding of, 70,
70f
proactive, development of,
68–73
selecting and implementing,
xxvii
technology as driver of, 33–35
understanding, 18

Sun Zi, 14
Supply chain, reinvention of, 159
Symbolic analysts. See Knowledge
workers

T
T/1 or T/3 lines, definition of, 175
Taco Bell, 154
Tagging, for electronic searches,
91–92, 91t
TechKNOWvation, 14
Technology. See also Communica-
tion(s)
adoption, natural acceleration
of, 61–62
breakthrough thinking about,
19–20
as driver of strategy, 33–35
innovation in, importance of,
7–8
obsolete businesses and, 38–40
rapid change in, 7
scanning for, 18
smart
in houses, 74–75
new value in, 4
as profit opportunity, 76–78,
77f
in real-time pricing, 146
ubiquitous, invisibility of, 76–77
understanding, 18
and writing, 4–5
Technology-enabled business strategy, critical drivers of, 33–35
Technotainment, 153–154
Telecommuting, impact of, 101
Telephone
cellular
electronic payments and, 146
history of, 7

opportunities opened by, 75
history of, 7
Television, declining viewership, 42
Testing and evaluation, of innovations, 21
Thesauruses, in electronic searches, 90–91
Thinking
models of, in information age, 10–11
nonlinear, techniques for, 19–20
Thirty-six Digital Alchemy® Strategies
in Align step, 109–130
in Deliver step, 135–154
in Innovate step, 65–103
overview of, 13–16
in Understand step, 31–62
"Thirty-six Strategies" (Chinese proverbs), 14
Thomas Cook, Inc., 55
3-D interfaces, advantages of, 62, 88–89
3M Corporation, 67
Time magazine, 96
Timeliness, consumer preference for, 113
Tracking of Web content use, 91*t*
Training, continual, importance of, 117–119
Trane Corp., 80
Transition planning, 20–21
Trends, analysis of, 18–19
Truman, Harry, 14, 159
Turf, threats to, 71–72
TV Guide, 79

U
Understand step, xxvi, 15*f,* 18*f*

action stimulators for, 63
activities in, 17–19
best practice companies, 32
goal of, 17, 31–32
Thirty-six Digital Alchemy® Strategies in, 31–62
United Airlines, 125
URL (Universal Resource Locator), definition of, 176
US West, 55
USA Today, 144
USA Today NewsTracker, 81–82
User-friendly interfaces, advantages of, 61–62

V
Value. *See also* Collaborative value networks
as focus of business, 158–159
information as, 8–9
of innovation, measuring, 21
transparency of, in information age, 36–37, 66, 147
Value-Added Networks, customer feedback and, 54
Variable pricing, 11*f,* 144–145
Variety, consumer preference for, 113
Vending machines, smart, 146
Verbal expression, going beyond, 19
Villages, as knowledge repositories, 139–141
Virgin Atlantic Airways, 125
Virgin Entertainment Group (U.K.), 67
Virtual competitors, 9
Virtual reality
advantages of, 62, 88–89
definition of, 176

Virtual workspaces. *See* Collaborative virtual workspaces
Vision
  implementation of, 21–22
    evaluating needs for, 20–21
  importance of, 13, 158

W
Wang, Tom, 97
Weaknesses, identifying, approaches for, 68–73
Wealth of Nations (Smith), 121
Web-time management
  in information age, 11*f*
  need for, 158–159
Wired, 18–19, 86, 169
Wireless communication
  impact of, 34, 34*t*
  leveraging of, 74–75
  privacy and, 34
The Work of Nations: Preparing Ourselves for 21st Century Capitalism (Reich), 121–122
Work teams, self-directed, 112
World Builder, Inc., 62
World Trade Center attack, impact of, 158
World Wide Web (WWW). *See also* Internet
  definition of, 176
  directory services on, 79–80
  history of, 7
  republishing content on, 91*t*, 92, 92*f*
  volume of use, 32
  Web sites
    on business news, 170
    business-to-business, 165–166
    business-to-consumer, 167–168
    capabilities *vs.* paper, 83–84
    government-to-constituent, 168
    industry information, 168–169
    interactive, benefits of, 53–55
    linking Web sites to, 91
    on marketing, 169–170
    personalization of, 84
    on research, 169
WorldWide Access, 67
Writing, technology and, 4–5
WWW. *See* World Wide Web

X
XML (eXtensible Markup Language)
  capabilities of, 91–92, 91*t*–92*t*
  definition of, 35
  impact of, 34*t*, 35

Y
Yahoo, 66–67, 79–80

Z
ZDNet, 169

About the Author

Eric Marcus is an internationally known strategist and futurist. As a sought-after keynote speaker and seminar leader or consulting with a select group of global, forward-thinking organizations, he provides insight and vision regarding the business impact of technology-enabled business strategies. Mr. Marcus also provides highly personalized executive one-on-one coaching. He works closely with client executives to develop multiyear business visions that are integrated with their overall business objectives and provide immediate, measurable results.

Industries Covered
Mr. Marcus's advisory relationships have included the pharmaceutical, chemical, airline, financial services, insurance, high tech-

nology, utilities, energy and natural resources, communications, retail, and publishing industries.

Professional Background

Prior to founding Corporate Alchemy, Mr. Marcus was president of The Concours Group's eBusiness Center of Excellence where he founded and led the firm's wide-ranging eBusiness strategy and research practice. Previously, he was vice president, CSC Index Research and Advisory Services, and executive director of its Vanguard program, where he led this global, multiclient strategic technology service. Previously, he was chief technology officer for Commerce Clearing House (CCH), a Fortune 500 publishing company, where he was responsible for worldwide information systems, commercial software development, and support and electronic publishing technologies. He also served as the chief operating officer for FDSI/Corptax, a national tax software company, managed the West Region Advanced Technology Consulting practice for Coopers & Lybrand, and practiced technology law.

Communications & Attributions

Mr. Marcus is an internationally recognized speaker on topics such as "Breakthrough Strategic Thinking," "Beyond the Net: The Next Strategic Technologies to Shape Business Competition," "Digital Cash: How Will It Reshape The Way We Do Business?", "Business Challenges in a Digital World," "Technology-Enabled Competitive Advantage," and "Critical Trends in the 21st Century: A Backdrop For Business Planning." He has also served as a member of the London Business School's global expert panel on future media and as a panelist for the National Academy of Sciences/National Research Council's "Technology Deployment for the National Information Infrastructure" program.

Mr. Marcus has been widely quoted in such media as *Wired*, *The Wall Street Journal*, *CIO Magazine*, *The Financial Review* (Aus), *The Australian* (Aus), *The Independent* (UK), and business bestseller *Webonomics*.

About the Author

His published articles include "From The Page To Online: Publishing In The Digital Age," "Knowledge Agents Aid in Research," "Using Memory Cards For Information Vending," and "Your Crystal Ball: A Guide to Future Real Estate Trends." Mr. Marcus has also been a frequent guest lecturer in the graduate schools of business at the University of Chicago and DePaul University.

Education
Mr. Marcus holds a Bachelor's Degree in Mathematics from Occidental College and a J.D. from Loyola Law School.

518 S. Route 31, Suite 140
McHenry, IL 60050 USA
ekmarcus@corporatealchemy.com
www.corporatealchemy.com
847.604.8716
(Fax) 847.604.8717